OXFORD

Encounters through History

HERITAGE HUNTER

Edited by
ANDREW CHAPMAN

This arrangement copyright © 2021 by Heritage Hunter
All rights reserved.

No part of this book may be reproduced in any form or by any electronic or mechanical means, including information storage and retrieval systems, without written permission from the author, except for the use of brief quotations in a book review.

www.heritagehunter.co.uk

Contents

To Helen, Paul and Helen

Introduction

Oxford is a city which has loomed large in British history through the influence of the university and its alumni, and the city itself has a rich and complex history, both in relation to the university and as a separate entity, including an industrial role from the 20th century.

There are countless journals, diaries, letters, memoirs and reminiscences by residents of, students at and visitors to Oxford reflecting on different aspects of the city, and this book can only offer a selection. The aim is to provide a representative sample from topographers, travellers, insiders and outsiders, particularly where their observations are unusual, original or entertaining. An entire volume could be filled with near-identical passages listing the university colleges and their respective histories, some more accurate than others, but only a few examples of those are here, in order to allow space for the rich variety of Oxford life and its people to come across. Some texts document how little Oxford has changed; others how much.

Common themes inevitably emerge down the ages – the questionable weather, the drunkenness of students (and dons), the beauties of the architecture, and sometimes there are challenges to the city's boasts. The aim is to ensure that every writer had actually been there, whether on the day of writing or at an earlier time, and that their accounts should be authentic. Frederick Raumer, whose letters home to Germany were published as *England in 1835*, commented: "No person should give an opinion of Oxford, its scientific, political, and ecclesiastical position, who has not seen it."

Many writers have rhapsodised, in increasingly repetitive ways, about the dreaming spires, but not everyone has been so impressed. Louis Simond (whose *Journal of a Tour and Residence in Great Britain by a French Traveller* (during 1810 and 1811) was published in English in 1815, commented: "The first sight of this great university, the antique seat of science, renowned for the splendour of its public edifices, did not answer our expectations. It looked old, dusty, and worm eaten—the streets silent and deserted,—a few students walking lazily…"

Sometimes great writers have been omitted due to the huge extent of their Oxford writings, or even their brevity. (Here's a nice line from a letter by Keats in 1817, for example: "For the last five or six days we have had regularly a boat on the Isis, and explored all the streams about, which are more in number than your eyelashes.")

In general, extensive histories have been left out in favour of travelogues, topographies and anecdotes, but overall there are many snippets and summaries of Oxford history to be found accumulated in these pages.

The book begins with the father of topography and antiquarianism, John Leland, not least because so many later writers drew upon his work. That work was a mixture of ferreting in libraries (many swept away by his patron Henry VIII) and real visits to the places in question. And he is followed by William Camden, who was perhaps more bookish still (and used Leland as a major source himself), but who certainly also travelled to many places, including Oxford, and again is an *ur*-source for others. Later Oxford historians, such as Anthony Wood and Thomas Hearne, are represented here, but only briefly and not for their formal histories.

Travel writing as a genre in itself took off in the 18th

century, and here there are numerous, but hopefully sufficiently varied, reports of visits to Oxford; likewise there are a few representative examples from the many topographical writers of the late 19th and early 20th centuries, some of whom took to the developing railway network to visit the places they wrote about.

The other 'bookend' for the selections here is Arthur Mee, whose team swarmed across the country by motor car to research the *King's England* series, which I'd argue remains the most comprehensive account of British history and heritage ever compiled, and offers a final historical snapshot before the ravages of the Second World War (and 1960s architects). The *Oxfordshire* volume has more than 280 pages detailing Oxford's history and sights – far too many to include here (his introductory text included here offers a separate and slightly different snapshot). These are now available in a reissued form as a companion to this book, *Historic Oxford.*

Note: In general the texts here are as they were published, in the editions referenced, sometimes with minor editing of punctuation or paragraph breaks for clarity. This is not intended as a work of academic rigour, but of general interest to bring five centuries of Oxford writing alive.

John Leland, c.1542-3

John Leland (c.1503–52) was the founding father of English topography, and the first person to call himself an antiquarian. He studied at Cambridge but according to tradition became a fellow of All Souls in Oxford. After the Dissolution of the Monasteries by Henry VIII, he undertook a series of 'itineraries' across England and Wales between 1538 and around 1543. His notes on these, and other writings, were first published in the 18th century and then in an authoritative, five-volume series from 1907–10, *The Itinerary of John Leland in or about the years 1535–1543*, edited by Lucy Toulmin Smith, from which the selections below are taken.[1] The precise dates of the itineraries are debated, but he is known to have been in Oxfordshire in 1542, and travelled westward in that year. The Roman numerals used here refer to the different Parts of Toulmin Smith's edition.

II

From Haseley *[where Henry VIII gave Leland the rectorship]* to Oxford about a 7 miles.

Robertas de Oilleio that cam into England with Wylliarn Conqueror had given to hym the baronyes of Oxford and Sainct Waleries.

This Robert made the castelle of Oxford, and, as I conject, other made the waulles of Oxford or repairid them.

This Robert made the chapelle of S. George in the castelle of Oxforde, and foundid a college of prebendaries there.

This Robert dyid withowt issue, and wher he was buried it is not very certeinly knowen.

This Robert had one John de Einerio that was exceding familiar with hym, and had beene in the warres as sworen brother onto hym, and had promised to be part taker of Robertes fortunes. Wherapon he enrichid hym with possessions, and, as sum think, gave hym S. Waleries.

Robert Oilley had a brother caullid Nigellus, of whom be no verye famose thinges written.

Nigellus had a sunne caullid Robert that provid a very noble man.

This Robert the 2. had a wife caullid Edith Forne, a woman of fame and highly estemid with King Henry the [first] by whose procuration Robert weddid her.

This Robert began the priorie of blake chanons at Oseney a by Oxford emong the isles that Isis ryver ther makith.

Sum write that this was the occasion of making of it. Edith usid to walk out [of] Oxford Castelle with her gentilwomen to solace and that often tymes, wher yn a certen place in a tre as often as she came a certen pies usid to gether to it, and ther to chattre, and as it wer to speke onto her. Edithe much marveling at this matier, and was sumtyme sore ferid as by a wonder.

Wherapon she sent for one Radulph, a chanon of S. Fredis-wides, a man of a vertuus life and her confessor, asking hym counsel: to whom he answerid, after that he had scene the fascion of the pies chattering only at her cumming, that she should builde sum chirch or monasterie in that place.

Then she entreatid her husband to build a priorie, and so he did, making Radulp the first prior of it.

The cumming of Edith to Oseney and Radulph waiting on her, and the tre with the chattering pies be paintid in the waulle of tharch over Edith tumbe in Oseney priorie.

There lyith an image of Edithe of stone in thabbite of a wowes, holding an hart in her right bond, on the north side of the high altare.

Robert Oilley the 2., founder of Oseney priorie, was buried in thabbay of Eignesham a a 3. miles from Oxford.

Robert Oilley the 2. had faire issue by Edith his wife, emong the which Henry was his heire.

This Henry lyith buried yn Oseney chirch, in the veri midle of the presbyteri, under a flatte marble stone, wherapon is a flourid cross porturid. This Henry had Henry the 2. And from Henry the 2. were other discentes; but in processe the landes of the Oilleys were disparkelid.

Ther is at this tyme one of the Oilleis a man of a 140. li. land dwelling…

This Oilley hath to wife my Ladie Williams doughter of Ricote.

He is now communely caullid Doilley of this title de Oilleio.

Ela, Countes of Warwik, a woman of a very great riches and nobilite, lyith buried at the hedde of the tumbe of Henry Oilley, undre a very fair flat marble, in the habite of a woues, graven yn a coper plate.

Ela gave many rich jewelles to Oseney, but no landes.

Ela gave sum landes to Royle b abbay by Oseney.

Ela gave riche giftes to thabbay of Reading.

On the north side of the presbyteri of Oseney chirch is buried undre an arche John Saincte John a famose man in an high and large tumbe of marble.

S. John's wife lyith under a flat marble by her husbandes tumbe.

Beaufort a knight lyith in the quier at the hed of Countes Ela.

This Bewfort and an abbate of Oseney buildid the body Oxon. of the chirch now standing at Oseney, and ther be porturid their images in the volt of it.

There be very faire doble isles on eche side of the body of the chirch.

There is buried at Oseney yn our Lady chapelle a noble man of the Placetes, in a faire tumbe with an image.

One Thomas Kidlington, borne at Kidlington in Oxfordshir, abbate of Oseney, buildid many yeres sins the chapelle of our Lady on the north side of the presbyterie of Oseney chirch.

There were in the beginning certen priors at Oseney: and then the rulers of the house were made abbates: at the which tyme the landes of Oseney were augmentid and partely given with a certen peculiar jurisdiction spiritual yn Glocestreshir.

One Mr. James Bayllie of Oxford hath a peace of a booke of the actes of the abbates of Oseney.

From Oxford thorough the southgate and bridge of sundrie arches over Isis, and along causey in ulter. ripa in Barkshir by a good quarter of a mile or more, and so up to Berks. Hinxey a hille, about a mile from Oxford.

From this place the hilly grounde was meately wooddy for the space of a mile: and thens 10. miles al by chaumpain, and sum corne, but most pasture, to Farington, standing in a stony ground in the decline of an hille.

X

From Oxford to Hinkesey fery a quartar of a myle or more. Ther is a cawsey of stone fro Oseney to the ferie, and in this cawsey be dyvers bridges of plankes. For there the streme of Isis breketh into many armelets. The fery selfe is over the principale arme or streame of Isis.

XI

The Universite Churche in Oxford, alias S. Marye Universite Churche, was begon to be reedified in the tyme of Doctor Churche in Fitz-James, aftar Bysshope of London. He procuryd muche Oxford mony towards the buyldynge of it. The enbatylments of it wer full of pinacles: but in a tempestious wethar most parte of them were throwne downe in one nyght…

There were in Oxford of auncient tyme 800. burgeses Oxforde. houses and mo with in the towne of Oxford, and a 400. without in the suburbes.

The scale of Oxford hathe an ox on it withe a castle, or wallyd towne, and about it is writen *Sigillum civitatis Oxoniae* etc.

Some say that there were 24. parishe churchis and mo in the towne and suburbs of Oxford.

Kynge Henry the first somewhat restoryd the towne of Oxforde.

The towne of Oxford moste floryshed withe scollars in an huge nombar, and other inhabitaunts, in Henry the 3. tyme. Ther was an infinit nombar of writars and parchement makers in Oxford in Henry the 3. tyme.

The bowrgesis of Oxford say that Vortimer made theyr fo. 1143. towne. The nombar of scolars and inhabitaunts in Oxforde were so greate in Henry the 3. tyme that they had lybertye to provyd for vitails 2. myles about.

Bridgs on Charwell.

Est Bridge at Oxford. To Iselep Brige of stone a 3. myles upper on Charwell by land. To Gosford Bridge a myle or more. To Emmeley a Bridge a 2. myles upper. To Hey wood b Bridge a 2. miles uper etc.

Where as now the bridge of stone is ovar Charwell by

Magdalen Colledge was a trajectus, or fery, in Kynge Henry the third's dayes, caulyd Steneford.

[Fragment]

Rosamundes tumbe at Godestow nunnery was taken up a late, it at [had?]* a stone, with this inscription, Tumba Rosa- mundae, her bones were closid in lede, and with yn that the bones were closid yn leder. When f it was openid ther was a uery swete [smell] cam owt of it.

Ther is a crosse hard by Godestow with this inscription, Qui meat hac oret signum salutis adoret Utque sibi detur veniam Rosamunda precetur.

---

1. The only modern edition is John Chandler's *John Leland's Itinerary: Travels in Tudor England* (1993; revised 1998), rendered in modern English and rearranged for clarity.

William Camden, 1590s

William Camden (1551–1623) was an antiquarian who, in his *Britannia*, provided the first systematic topographical and historical survey of Great Britain, relating the nation's past to its (then) present. Although his work draws considerably on John Leland's, he is known to have undertaken considerable fieldwork, including a visit to Oxford in 1596. Britannia went through multiple editions from 1586 (in Latin) to 1607, and was translated into English by Philemon Holland in 1610; the text below is from Edmund Gibson's expanded edition of 1695.

But where the Cherwel[l] flows along with the Isis, and their divided streams make several little sweet and pleasant islands, is seated on a rising vale the most famous University of *Oxford*, in Saxon *Oxenford*, our most noble *Athens*, the seat of the English Muses, the prop and pillar, nay the sun, the eye, the very soul of the nation: the most celebrated fountain of wisdom and learning, from whence Religion, Letters, and good Manners, are happily diffus'd thro' the whole Kingdom. A delicate and most beautiful city, whether we respect the neatness of private buildings, or the stateliness of publick structures, or the healthy and pleasant situation. For the plain on which it stands is walled in, as it were, with hills of wood, which keeping out on one side the pestilential south-wind, on the other, the tempestuous west, admit only the purifying east, and the north that disperses all unwhol[e]some vapours. From which delightful situation, Authors tell us it was heretofore call'd *Bellositum.* some writers fancy this city, in the British times, had the name of *Caer Vortigern* and *Caer-Vember,* and was built by God knows what *Vortigerns* or *Memprics.* Whatever it was under the Britains, it is certain the Saxons call'd it Oxenford, in the same meaning, no doubt, as the Grecians had their *Bosphorus,* and the Germans their *Ochenfurt* upon the river *Oder*; that is, *a ford of Oxen.* In which sense it is still call'd by the Welsh *Rhid-Ychen.* Yet Mr. Leland, with some shew of probability, derives the name from the river *Ous,* in Latin *Isis,* and believes it to have been heretofore call'd *Ousford,* especially since the little islands which the river here makes, are call'd *Ousney* [i.e. Osney].

Wise Antiquity (as we read in our Chronicles) even in the British age, consecrated this place to the Muses, whom they transplanted hither, as to a more fertile nursery, from *Greek-lade,* now a small town in Wiltshire… But in the following Saxon age, remarkable for the continual ruin and subversion of towns and cities, this place underwent the common fate; and during many years, was famous for nothing but the reliques of St *Frideswide*, a virgin of great esteem for the sanctity of her life, and first reputed a saint on this occasion; that when by a solemn vow she had devoted her self to the service of God and a single life, Earl *Algar* courted her for a wife, and pursuing her in her flight, was miraculously (as the story goes) struck blind. *This Lady* (as we read in William of Malmesbury) *built here a Religious house as a trophy of her preserv'd virginity, into which Monastery, when in the time of Ethelred several Danes sentenc'd to death were fled for refuge, the enraged Saxons burnt them and the house together. But afterwards the penitent King cleans'd the sanctuary, rebuilt the Monastery, restor'd the old endowment, and added new possessions: and at last Roger Bishop of Salisbury gave the place to a very learned Canon Regular, who there set[t]led a perpetual society of such Regular Canons for the service of God.*

But leaving these matters, let us return to the University. The Danish storms being pretty well blown over, the pious Prince K. Aelfred restor'd the Muses (who had suffer'd a long exile) to their former habitation, and built three Colleges, one for Grammarians, another for Philosophers, and a third for Divinity…

… in the reign of K. Etheldred, the Danes sack'd and burn'd the city. And soon after, Harold surnam'd Harefoot, was so incens'd against the place for the death of some of his friends in a tumult, and prosecuted his revenge in so barbarous a manner, that the scholars were miserably banish'd from their studies, and the University, a sad spectacle, lay as it were expiring till the time of the Conquerour; when too (as some say) he besieg'd and took this city: but those who write so, have been impos'd upon by reading in faulty copies *Oxonia* instead of *Exonia.* Yet… it was even then a place of study…

… about this time the city was so impoverish'd, that whereas (according to the general survey) there were reckon'd within and without the walls 750 houses, besides 24 mansions upon the walls, 500 of 'em were not able to pay the geld or tax. When (to speak from the authority of Domesday-book) this city *paid for toll and gable and other customs, yearly to the King, twenty pounds and six sextaries of honey, and to Earl Algar ten pounds.* soon after, *Robert de Oili,* a noble Norman before-mention'd, when for the reward of his services he had received from the Conquerour a large portion of lands in this county, he built a castle on the west-side of the City, fortified with large trenches and rampires, and in it a Parish-Church dedicated to St George; to which the Parishioners not having free access, when the Empress Maud was closely besieg'd in this castle by King Stephen, the Chapel of St Thomas hard by was built for that purpose. He is supposed likewise to have beautified the city with new walls, which are now by age sensibly impair'd. Robert his Nephew, son of his brother Nigel, Chamberlain to King Hen. I by persuasion of his wife *Edith,* daughter of *Furn,* who had been the last Concubine of that Prince, in the island meadows nigh the castle, built *Oseny* Abby, which the ruins of the walls still shew to have been very large.

... *John Rous* of Warwick writes thus. *By the care of King Henry the first, the Lecture of Divinity, which had been long intermitted, began again to flourish, and this Prince built there a new Palace, which was afterward converted by King* Edward II *into a Convent for Carmelite Friers.* But long before this conversion, was born in that Palace the truly Lion-hearted Prince, King *Richard* I commonly call'd *C[o]eur de Lion...*

The City being thus adorn'd with beautiful buildings, many students began to flock hither as to the common Mart of civility and good letters. so that learning here quickly reviv'd, chiefly through the care of the foresaid *Robert Pulein,* a man born to promote the interest of the learned world, who spar'd no trouble and pains to cleanse and open the fountains of the Muses (which had been so miserably dried and damm'd up) under the favour and protection of King *Henry* I. King *Henry* II and *Richard* his son, whom I mention'd just before. And he met with such fortunate success in his endeavours, that in the reign of King *John,* there were three thousand students in this place, who went away altogether, some to *Reading,* and some to *Cambridge*, when they could no longer bear the abuses of the rude and insolent Citizens: but when these tumults were appeas'd, they soon after return'd. Then and in the following times, as Divine Providence seem'd to set apart this City for a seat of the Muses, so did the same Providence raise up a great number of excellent Princes and Prelates, who exercis'd their piety and bounty in this place for the promoting and encouraging of Arts and all good Literature. And when King *Henry* III came hither and visited the shrine of s. *Frideswide,* which was before thought a dangerous crime in any Prince, and so took away that superstitious scruple, which had before hind[e]red several Kings from ent[e]ring withlin the walls of *Oxford:* He here conven'd a Parliament to adjust the differences between him and the Barons, and at that time confirm'd the privileges granted to the University by his

Predecessors, and added some new acts of grace and favour. After which the number of learned men so far encreas'd, as to afford a constant supply of persons qualified by divine and humane knowledge for the discharge of offices in Church and state.

… one may easily observe, that *Oxford* was the chief school in England, Scotland, Wales and Ireland… For the name of *University* for publick schools of Learning, obtain'd first about the reign of King *Henry* III and, if I am not mistaken, this word did not at first so much signifie the place of study, as the society of students. But perhaps this may seem out of my road.

Now the worthy Patrons and Favourers of Learning began to furnish the City and suburbs with stately Colleges, Halls, and schools, and to endow them with ample Revenues, (for before this time the greatest part of the University stood without North-gate.) Then in the reign of King *Henry* III *John Baliol* of *Bernard*-castle, who died in the year 1269. Father of *John Baliol* King of *scots*, founded *Baliol*-College. And soon after *Walter Merton*, Bishop of *Rochester*, transferr'd the College which he had built in *Surrey*, to *Oxford* in the year 1274, endow'd, it and call'd it *Merton*-College. Then *William* Archdeacon of *Durham* repair'd and restor'd the Foundation of King *Alfred*, which we now call *University*-College. About which time the scholars having been somewhat rude to *Otto* the Pope's Legate, (or rather his Horse-leach, sent hither to suck the blood of the poor people) they were excommunicated, and treated with great severity. At which time, as *Richard* of *Armagh* tells us, there were reckon'd in this University no less than thirty thousand students. Under King *Edward* the second, *Walter Stapledon* Bishop of *Exeter* built *Exeter*-College and *Hart*-Hall; and the King, after his example, a Royal College, commonly call'd *Orial*, and St *Mary*-Hall… After this Queen *Philippa* wife of King *Edward* III built *Queens*-College: and *Simon Islip* Arch-bishop of *Canterbury*, *Canterbury*-College. The scholars now abounding in peace and plenty, grew insolent upon their good fortune, and divided into the factions of the Northern and southern men, carrying on the quarrel with open arms and all manner of hostility; upon which the Northern-men retir'd to *Sta[m]ford*, and there set up publick schools.

But after a few years, when the storm was blown over, and the feuds forgot, they all return'd hither again, and statutes were enacted to prohibit all persons from professing at *Stamford* to the prejudice of *Oxford*. About that time *William Wickam*, Bishop of *Winchester*, built a magnificent structure call'd *New* College, into which the ripest Lads are every year transplanted from his other College at *Winchester*. Then *Richard Angervil*, Bishop of *Durham*, calld *Philobiblos*, or The Lover of Books, began a publick Library. And his successor *Thomas de Hatfield* built *Durham*-College for the benefit of the Monks of *Durham:* and *Richard Fleming*, Bishop of *Lincoln*, founded *Lincoln*-College. About the same time the Benedictine Monks built *Glocester*-College at their own proper cost and charges, where were constantly maintain'd two or three Monks of every House of that Order, who afterwards should profess good Letters in their respective Convents. To speak nothing of the Canons of St *Frideswide*, there were erected no less than four beautiful Cells of Friers in the suburbs, where there often flourish[ed] men of considerable parts and learning. In the next age, during the reign of King Henry V *Henry Chichely* Archbishop of *Canterbury*, founded two eminent Colleges; one of which he dedicated to the memory of *All-Souls*, and the other to St *Bernard*. Not long after *William Wainster*, Bishop of *Winchester*, built *Magdalen*-College, remarkable for building, fine situation, and pleasure of adjoining groves and walks. At the same time the *Divinity School* was erected...

And above this school was a Library furnisht with one hundred twenty nine choice Volumes procur'd from *Italy* at the great expense of *Humphrey the Good*, Duke of *Glocester*, a chief Patron and admirer of Learning. But most of these Books are long since embezell'd and converted to private uses. But now (may all happiness attend the generous design) the worthy Sir *Thomas Bodley* Kt. formerly a Member of this University, with extraordinary charge, and indefatigable pains, is furnishing a new Library in the same place with the best Books procur'd from all parts of the world: that the University may enjoy a publick Arsenal of Wisdom, and he himself an everlasting honour. And since it was a good custom of the Ancients in all their Libraries to erect statues of Gold, silver, or Brass, both to those who had instituted them, and those who had adorn'd them with excellent Writings, that time and Age might not triumph over Benefactors, and that the curiosity of Mankind might be satisfied, while they enquired after men of worth and publick spirit: For this reason the present Chancellor of the University, at the same time providing for the memorial of himself, has in this Library erected a statue of Sir *Thomas Bodley*...

In the Reign of Henry the seventh, for the better advancement of Learning, *William Smith* Bishop of *Lincoln*, built new out of the Ground *Brazen-Nose*-College, which was well endow'd by the pious and good old man *Alexander Nowell* Dean of St *Pauls*. About the same time *Richard Fox*, Bishop of *Winchester*, founded *Corpus-Christi*-College. After these, Cardinal *Wolsey* Archbishop of *York*, on the site of the Monastery of St *Frideswide*, began the most noble and ample Foundation of all others, which King *Henry* VIII with addition of *Canterbury*-College, did richly endow, and gave it the name of *Christ-Church*. The same mighty Prince, at the expense of his own Exchequer, honoured the City with an Episcopal see, and the University with publick Professors. And in our own age, that the Muses might still be courted with greater favours, Sir *Thomas Pope* Kt. and Sir *Thomas White* Kt. Citizen and Alderman of London, have repair'd *Durham* and *Bernard* Colleges (which lay almost buried in their own dust,) have enlarg'd their buildings, endow'd them with lands, and given them new names, dedicating the former to the *Holy Trinity*, this latter to St *John Baptist*. Queen *Mary* built from the ground the publick schools. And lately *Hugh Price* Dr. of Laws, has happily laid a new foundation call'd in honour of our saviour, *Jesus*-College. These Colleges in number sixteen, beside eight Halls, all fairly built, and well endow'd, together with their excellent and useful Libraries, do so raise the credit and esteem of

Oxford, that it may be justly thought to exceed all other Universities in the world.

… The Astronomers observe this City to be in twenty two degrees of longitude or distance from the fortunate Islands; and in the northern latitude of fifty one degrees and fifty minutes.

Paul Hentzner, 1598

Paul Hentzner (1558–1623) was a German lawyer who set out on a tour of switzerland, France, England and Italy in 1597. He first published an account of his travels, in Latin, in 1612, and an English translation was made by the classical scholar Richard Bentley, published in 1757. Large chunks of Hentzner's work are clearly 'borrowed' from William Camden and according to W.D. Robson-Scott,[1] "Hentzner's own experiences in England form only a very small section of the whole". (The text below is from an 1892 edition, *Travels in England during the Reign of Queen Elizabeth.*)

[Most of Hentzner's description of Oxford is very similar to Camden's. But he adds this note about student life.]

These students lead a life almost monastic; for as the monks had nothing in the world to do but when they had said their prayers at stated hours to employ themselves in instructive studies, no more have these. They are divided into three tables: the first is called the Fellows' table, to which are admitted earls, barons, gentlemen, doctors, and Masters of Arts, but very few of the latter—this is more plentifully and expensively served than the others; the second is for Masters of Arts, Bachelors, some gentlemen, and eminent citizens; the third for people of low condition. While the rest are at dinner or supper in a great hall, where they are all assembled, one of the students reads aloud the Bible, which is placed on a desk in the middle of the hall, and this office every one of them takes upon himself in his turn. As soon as grace is said after each meal, every one is at liberty either to retire to his own chambers or to walk in the College garden, there being none that has not a delightful one. Their habit is almost the same as that of the Jesuits, their gowns reaching down to their ankles, sometimes lined with fur; they wear square caps. The doctors, Masters of Arts, and professors, have another kind of gown that distinguishes them. Every student of any considerable standing has a key to the College library, for no college is without one.

In an out-part of the town are the remains of a pretty large fortification, but quite in ruins. We were entertained at supper with an excellent concert, composed of a variety of instruments.

---

1. 'some notes on Hentzner's "Itinerarium"', *The Modern Language Review*, Vol. 46, No. 3/4 (Jul. - Oct., 1951), pp. 458-461.

Baron Waldstein, 1600

Baron Waldstein (Zdeněk Brtnický z baron Valdštejna, 1581–1623) was a Moravian nobleman who toured Europe, keeping a journal from 1597 to 1623. His journal of a visit to England – at the age of 19 – was translated by G.W. Groos and published as The Diary of Baron Waldstein in 1981. The original Latin manuscript is in the Vatican Library.

Oxford has the most famous university in England… It is a noble and distinguished city from every point of view, whether you have in mind the beauty of its private buildings, or the dignity of its public ones, or the healthiness and charm of its situation. Wooded hills make a rampart about its level plain, protecting it on the one side from the plague-bearing south wind, and on another from the stormy west, but leaving it open to the east wind which brings fine weather, and to the north which keeps away infectious diseases.

[Waldstein gives the early history of Oxford and list the colleges with details of their founding.]

SUNDAY, 16 JULY

The Vice-Chancellor of the University (the Chancellor is the Lord Admiral of England) came in person to visit us at our lodging in a procession led by 5 [Beadles], after he had read a letter in which we were given an introduction by the Cambridge Vice-Chancellor. When he had greeted us he at once asked (for we were thinking of leaving on the following day) if we needed to go so soon, and would we not first see something of the work of the University. What was more, the yearly presentations and Assemblies were due to take place within the coming week. We discussed it from every angle and at last made up our minds to stay on for at least some time, so that same evening we sent Master Linyard the tailor on ahead to London with the horses.

Later the Vice-Chancellor took us to attend an Anglican service… After the service was over we went to Christ Church… Next we visited st John's College…

We were invited to dinner at the Vice-Chancellor's; the erudite and celebrated Rainolds was also present.

MONDAY, 17 JULY

Had lunch in Christ Church as guests of one of the Doctoral Candidates who greeted us as 'most noble kings'. There too we were splendidly entertained: not only was it a sumptuous meal, but, with the extreme courtesy which the English show, they invited us to lead the procession.

TUESDAY, 18 JULY

Visited Magdalen College, famous for its long and beautiful walk and for its unusually large grounds (it stands 80 yards from its gates). Next we went to the College of the Brazen Nose: it is this, attached to the College gates, which gives the place its name. From here we went to the Divinity school, which is extremely fine; it contains a high professorial chair made of stone.

Adjoining it there is a very beautiful library, the ceiling decorated with coats-of-arms and devices. Here the arms of the University are displayed: 3 crowns, a book with 2 seals, and the inscription 'Dominus illuminatio mea'. It has identical bookshelves on either side and two study.1 rooms. It was built by a private citizen of Oxford, Thomas Bodley; at his own expense he employs people in different parts of Europe and they collect choice books for the library here.

Since we had now made up our minds to wait for the day of the Oxford Assemblies, we went this evening to another lodging, a private hostel kept by a good fellow called Sherburn, and remained there, living on our own provisions, for the best part of a week.

WEDNESDAY, 19 JULY

Went this morning to Lincoln College. In the evening after dinner we went back to this college – it being in the same part of the town as our hostel – and listened to some very learned declamations and to the disputations they provoked.

THURSDAY, 20 JULY

This evening a very distinguished Italian, the Oxford Professor Alberic Gentilis, called on us; we then went out with him and enjoyed ourselves on a boating trip.

FRIDAY, 21 JULY

Went to All Souls' College where there is a collection of annotated manuscripts, and then to the Queen's College which has a cup made from a horn and decorated with silver-gilt rings. After this to Trinity College: here they have the alabaster tomb of Thomas Pope, knight, the founder of this College, together with that of his wife. We also visited Merton College: there are two departments in its library, one is for manuscripts only, the other for printed books. They have a book containing the names of all the Fellows of the College with the kings of England under whose reigns they lived…

SATURDAY, 22 JULY

The Commencement of the Oxford Assemblies. some excellent lectures were given during the morning by various Professors: we ourselves attended a lecture in Theology given by an extremely learned man named Holland. In the afternoon the Theological disputations took place. There were some really good declamations on the subject of Peregrination.

The Windischgraetzes joined us, and in the evening we took out a boat and enjoyed some music.

SUNDAY, 23 JULY

Lunched in Magdalen College. After going for a trip on the river we spent the evening with the Windischgraetzes.

MONDAY, 24 JULY

Another day of Assemblies, also the actual conferring of degrees, first the Masters and then the Doctors. In the evening we presented ourselves at Christ Church for the Doctoral dinner to which we had been invited.

Soon after midnight and by the light of the moon (it was quite impossible to ride by day as the weather was so unbearably hot) we left Oxford with the Windischgraetzes.

Frederic Gerschow, 1602

Frederic Gerschow (d.1635) was a professor of law at the University of Greifswald in Germany, and personal tutor and secretary to Philip Julius, the Duke of stettin-Pomerania. Gerschow accompanied the duke on a tour of England in september and October 1602, and kept a journal of their trip at the duke's instruction. It was translated into English in 1892.[1]

On the 24th, when we reached Oxford about midday, 10 miles, the road being very bad and marshy, we sent at once for the *supremo bibliothecario*, Mr. Thomas Gameth [James?], who showed us over the *Collegia academiae Oxoniensis*, 16 in number. He also showed us the 8 aulas [Latin for 'courtyards'] where every [student] may procure his meals for his own money, and pays about 5 *orthsthaler* a week for his board. In the colleges the *stipendiata* live *communi sumptu*.

[Gerschow lists the 16 colleges in Latin with their founding dates.]

… As his princely Grace remained in the Collegio Regali for some little time, a professor presented himself, accompanied by a beadle, bearing a silver sceptre, and bade his Highness welcome.

The *bibliothecario* also was ordered to show everything to his Grace.

The *auditorium publicum* is a fine building of square stones, and in fact all the colleges in Oxford are built *ex vivo lapide* at an incredible expense, there being no good quarry in the whole kingdom.

In the upper hall there was an *instructissima bibliotheca* in all the various languages and manuscripts to be found in the whole world.

This university has many precious *privilegia* – for instance, that even the royal governor is obliged to swear the oath anew every year to the *procancellario*, who acts as rector.

Six sceptres are borne before the *procancellario*, three golden by the *pedellibus nobilibus*, and three silver ones by the *plebejis*.

... In the evening, whilst we were at table, the *procancellarius* presented his Highness *per pedellum nobilem* with a Latin *epistolam cum hac inscriptione*: 'Illustri hospite ignoto,' together with a beautiful pair of gloves, embossed in gold, and a tankard of good wine.

---

1. 'Diary of the Journey of Philip Julius, Duke of stettin-Pomerania, through England in the Year 1602', *Transactions of the Royal Historical society*, 1892, Vol. 6 (1892), pp. 1-67.

Sir Roger Wilbraham, 1603

Sir Roger Wilbraham (1553–1616) was an English lawyer who served under both Elizabeth I and James I. His journal from 1593 to 1616 survives – *The Journal of Sir Roger Wilbraham* was published in 1902.

Monday 9 Sept.: I was at Oxford; wher lying at the Crosse Inne the best in the citie, yet was ther two howses on either side adjoining infected with plague: *sed deus nos protegat.*

There was the Spanishe Ambassador lodged in Christchurch and the Archduke's Ambassador lodged in Mawdelin Colledge: the attended ther audience at the king's coming to Wodstock.

I surveyed the chiefest colledges: 1° Christchurch which was ment to have ben a famous monument, but never finished by the founder Cardinall Wolsey… Mawdelins is the second chief colledge… ther are walkes sufficient to environ a litle towne: for besides a close of X acres walled about for walkes & severall divided walks with ash trees, they have manie orchards walled in, & ech chamber to 2 Fellows have a peculiar orcharde.

They have walkes also made in the medowes wherin the river of Temmies, & of Charwell do runne & meete; invironed close walk of willow & some elmes, to walk the distance of half a mile, in shadowes: this is the most compleet & fairest colledg & walks in England: (tho Trinitie CoUedg square is much larger & fairer.)

... Oxford stands lowe, with rich meadowes about the rivers that runne by it: & Oxford is invironed with pretie litle hills two miles off by south & west: that part northward a flatt: the soile is clay & sand: a lighter ground & mold.

Thomas Crosfield, 1636

Thomas Crosfield (1602–63), from Kendal, became a fellow of Queen's College, and later rector of Spennithorne in Yorkshire. His diary, published as *The Diary of Thomas Crosfield* in 1935, offers many details of social and university life in Oxford.

February 1

Seene a bull baiting in St Clement's, where the manner is thus; (i) The dogges, 10 or 12, are brought chained into the yard, where tyed, their anger or courage such as to bite or breake the chaines they are tyed with; (2) The Bull brought in with hornes buttened, & tied to the stake, walkes about, the dogs one at once set on: if he catch him above collar, chiefly by the nose, accounted victor. After all have played [one] round, they commonly have a second boute.

N.B. (i) 1 d. a piece for every person that goes in, & 2d. in a chamber; (2) The Bull Master may strike the doggs if two set on at a time.

February 2

By reason of the late taxation for ship money, some envious persons against the good government of his majestie, have dispersed the rumour in some places, market townes—that every woman wearing a greene apron must pay 4d., every one wearing a ring—to the King.

February 12

Some of Oxford cited to appeare personally at the Starre chamber for dressing meat upon fasting dayes, accused by some informers that take their oath they are guilty of the crimes laid against them, such were Dr King, Brise of the Crosse-Inne—one of the Red Lion—&c. These make some colourful pretences, as one for his parents of 80 yeares age, another for himselfe diseased—but commonly are deeply sessed & fined to the King.

Lieutenant Hammond (?), 1634

This extract comes from a journal undertaken in 1634 by "A captain, a lieutenant, and an ancient", all anonymous. The editor of the 1904 edition, *A short survey of 26 Counties*, suggests the lieutenant appears to have been the chief author, and his surname was possibly Hammond. The book recounts a seven-week trip across England, setting out from their military base in Norwich.

There *[in Oxford]* wee met, and noe sooner vayl'd our Bonnetts to each other, but I was summon'd by my noble Freind, the Gentleman whom I parted with this Morning, to a Briske Cup of the Muses Liquour. Whither also speedily came, a free, and true-hearted scholler (one that had a neere Relation to the generous, noble, and graue Lord Bishop) who at our setting out promis'd to meet us heere; indeed hee is one, who is so kind, and valiant, to fill up a military Messe, and to bee ycleeped Chaplain in our Travells, by whose good meanes, and for his noble Lords and Tutors sake, wee found a free, curteous, and generous entertainment, in a superlative manner, all the time of our abode there, both in the Colleges, and in the Towne, and kindly did they spend their labour and precious time, in shewing of us, all the sweet uniforme seats of their gloriously built Muses; their rich, and neat Chappells; and their rare, admir'd, and unparralell'd Library, most stately built for Publique use, which was erected by that pious, Learned, and worthy Knight of renowned Memory *[i.e. sir Thomas Bodley]*, and also every particular Collegiate Library; Their goodly large Halls, Cellers, and Buttryes, and in the last a fre[e] lasting taste of their generous, and free-hearted dispositions, whereof if I should relate all the particulers, with the pleasant scytuation of that famous *[Osney]* Abbey, etc. would add another taske thereto; therefore wee shall leave it to judicious Men, of worth, and quality who have beene the like participants with us, from these generous, and free-hearted Academians, and Brittish Muses, rightly, and duely, to judge, and relate.

Wee had but small time to walke the sweet City, for spending some time in their dainty walkes, the Organs, voyces, Monuments, and windowes, both of the Cathedrall, and euery other Collegiate Church, and Chappell, were soe fayre, sweet, rich, and glorious, as which exceeded each other, wee were not able to judge.

At this sweet Fountaine of Literature, wee stay'd longer then wee determin'd, by one whole naturall Day, and longer had we stay'd had we not us'd our martiall Power to march…

Robert Woodforde, 1639

Robert Woodforde (1606–54) was a lawyer and diarist who was steward of Northampton from 1635 onwards. His diary, which has survived from 1637 to 1641, provides an insight into the mind of a Puritan and records his thoughts as he travels between the Midlands and London in the lead-up to the Civil War. This pithy extract is from a selection published by the Historical Manuscripts Commission.[1]

July 9th. Went to Oxford.
July 10th. This place is prodigiously profane I perceive for drunkenness, swearing, and other debauched courses, stage plays, &c.

1. *Ninth Report*, Part II 1883-1884, pp. 496-499.

Anthony Wood, 1642

Anthony Wood (1632–95) was a noted antiquarian who lived and died in Oxford. His extensive diaries and memoirs were published in four volumes as The Life and Times of Anthony Wood between 1891 and 1900, and cover every aspect of life in Oxford in the 17th century. The short extracts here include his memories of the early stages of the English Civil War, when Oxford was at the heart of the Royalist cause – Wood himself was only nine years old at the time.

August, 1642. Upon the publication of His Majesty's Proclamation, for the suppression of the rebellion under command of Robert Devereux, Earl of Essex, the members of the University of Oxford began to put themselves in a posture of defence and especially for another reason, which was that there was a strong report that divers companies of soldiers were passing through the country, sent from London by the Parliament for the securing of Banbury and Warwick. My father had then armour for one man, viz. a helmet, a back and breast-piece, a pike and a musket, and other appurtenances. And the eldest of his men-servants, (for he had then three) named Thomas Burnham, did appear in those arms when the scholars and privileged men trained; and when he could not train, being taken up with business, the next servant did train; and much ado there was to keep Thomas Wood, the eldest son, then a student of Christ Church, from putting on the said armour and training among the scholars. And there was no holding the schoolboys in their school from seeing and following them; and I remember well that some young scholars could never be brought to their books again.

And then afterwards, upon Thursday, being the 18th of August, in the afternoon, all those scholars and privileged men marched from the schools, all along up the High street, to the number of 330 or more, to Christ Church College, where they were put into array and a little exercised; and about 4 or 5 o'clock, it beginning to rain, they marched back again the same way to the schools; and so they departed for that time.

The Saturday following, they met at the schools again in the fore noon; from whence they marched down through Holywell, and so through a gate near Mr. Napper's house, they entered into New Park; where, by their commanders, they were divided into four squadrons, whereof two of them were musketeers, the third was a squadron of pikes, the fourth of halberds; and after they had been reasonably instructed in the words of command and in their postures, they were put into battle array, and skirmished together in a very decent manner; and continuing there until about 2 of the clock in the afternoon, they returned, entering into the town at St Giles his church, and so to Bocardo, they came marching all the way through the market place, and so over Carfax, and down the High street, and so they arrived at the schools again, from whence they were dismissed for that time. The scholars were Graduates and Undergraduates; a great many of them Masters of Art, yea, divines also, and Dr. Read of New College, a Doctor of Law, served with a pike.

Sunday, October 23, 1642. The great fight at Edgehill in Warwickshire, between the armies of King Charles I and his Parliament was begun. Upon the first news at Oxford that the armies were going to fight, my eldest brother Thomas left his gown at the town's end; ran to Edgehill; did His Majesty good service; returned on horseback well accoutred, and afterwards was made an officer in the King's army.

This year Oxford was garrisoned for the King. The scholars were put out of their colleges, and those that remained bore arms for the King in the garrison.

October 29, 1642. The King's Majesty, towards the evening, came from Edgehill Battle, and from Banbury-side, to Oxford, in at the North Gate on horse-back, with his army of footmen; Prince Rupert and his brother Maurice, also the young Prince Charles and his brother the Duke of York; they lodged at Christ Church; the footmen were billeted in and about Oxford. They came in their full march into the town, with about 60 or 70 colours borne before them which they had taken at the said Battle of Edgehill from the Parliament's forces which they had vanquished upon Sunday, the 23rd of October. The Mayor and townsmen presented themselves to His Majesty at Penniless Bench, and presented him also with a sum of money, as I heard. The ordnance and great guns were driven into Magdalen College Grove, about 26 or 27 pieces, with all their carriages.

John Evelyn, 1654

John Evelyn (1620–1706) was a gardener and diarist, known for his account of the Great Fire of London and many other events of the 17th century, as well as numerous books and pamphlets. There are numerous editions of his selected diaries available.

July 12th. We went to St John's, saw the library and the two skeletons, which are finely cleansed and put together. Observable is here also the store of mathematical instruments, chiefly given by the late Archbishop Laud, who built here a handsome quadrangle.

Thence we went to New College, where the chapel was in its ancient garb, notwithstanding the scrupulosity of the times. Thence, to Christ's Church, in whose library was showed us an office of Henry VIII., the writing, miniatures, and guilding whereof is equal, if not surpassing, any curiosity I had seen of that kind ; it was given by their founder, Cardinal Wolsey. The glass windows of the cathedral (famous in my time) I found much abused. The ample hall and column, that spreads its capital to sustain the roof as one goes up the stairs, is very remarkable.

Next, we walked to Magdalen College, where we saw the library and chapel, which was likewise in pontifical order, the altar only I think turned tablewise, and there was still the double organ, which abominations (as now esteemed) were almost universally demolished; Mr. Gibbon, that famous musician, giving us a taste of his skill and talents on that instrument.

Hence, to the Physic Garden, where the sensitive plant was showed us for a great wonder. There grew canes, olive-trees, rhubarb, but no extraordinary curiosities, besides very good fruit, which, when the ladies had tasted, we returned in our coach to our lodgings.

Samuel de Sorbiere, 1664

Samuel de Sorbière (1615–70) was a French physician and a translator of English works of philosophy. He visited England in 1663–4, publishing a critical account of his stay which provoked angry responses and political tensions. (He speaks favourably of Oxford, however.) An English translation was published as *A Journey to England* in 1709.

… Mr. Lockey, the Oxford Librarian, who had learnt at Court and in France to put on an obliging Air, and courteous Behaviour… had the Goodness, not only to conduct me to the Library, but all the Colledges, and to introduce me to all the Professors I visited: I lodged in Christ-Church, which is the largest and richest Colledge of them all, its Income being 70000 Livres a Year: Cardinal Wolsey Built it in the Reign of Henry VIII. of whom he was such a Favourite, that that Prince Built Hampton-Court for him, which is now a Royal Palace, Twelve Miles from London: There are Seventeen or Eighteen Colleges at Oxford, which are almost all of the same Dimensions: They are Built of Free-Stone, the meanest of them is not Inferior to the Sorbonne, for there are some of them that do excel it. The lower Court of Christ-Church College is little less than that which is contained within the Barriers of the Place-Royale: There is a Physick-Garden over-against St Catherine's, towards the Gate that leads to London, which is small, ill kept, and more like an Orchard than a Garden.

I shall not take upon me to describe all the Colledges to you. There is one, at whose Gate I saw a great Brazen Nose, like Punchinello's Vizard: was told they also call it Brazen-Nose College, and that John Dunscotus taught here, in Remembrance of which they set up the Sign of his Nose at the Gate. The last College I visited was St John's, which is the most Regular Building of any of them, tho' not the Richest: It has Two Square Courts, as large as the Square we now have in the Louvre; and Two large Buildings Three Story high, with Four Wings of the same height: I saw a Fine Library in one of them, and a large Wainscotted Gallery, wherein found no other Ornament than the Picture of King Charles I. which they took out of a Cover, and and shewed here for a Rarity; because the Hair of his Head was made up of Scripture Lines, wrought wonderfully small, and more particularly of the Psalms of David in Latin. This Prince, and the Queen Mother's Statues in Brass, stand in the Second Court upon the Two Gates: and the Two late Archbishops of Canterbury, who were Benefactors to this College, are Buried in the Chapel: There are Two large Gardens belonging to this College, one of which is terrassed, and the other faces. a Plain to the Northward.

The Famous Library of the University of Oxford, where their Publick Lectures are read, requires we should dwell a long while upon it; but I had only a Transient View of it: It's made in the form of an H, has Two Stories of Books: The lowermost has Six Rows of Folio's, and Three of Quarto's: In the other, to which you go up by wooden Stairs, very artfully contrived for to give Light in the Middle, and at the Four Corners, there are Nine Rows more, whereof Three in Folio's, and the rest of different Volumes… Here is a Place of Anatomy not worth feeing: The Schools were all of them shut up; and there are scarce any Lectures read there, because the private ones draw all the Scholars thither.

Oxford City would be nothing without the Colleges; for there are scarce any more Inhabitants in it than are enough to serve Three or Four Thousand Students, and to cultivate a very delightful Plain, where the City stands upon small River, abounding with Fish, which falls near it into the Thames.

Sir John Lauder, 1667

Sir John Lauder (1646–1722), Lord Fountainhall, was a Scottish legal expert who kept diaries of his travels between 1665 and 1676, published as Journals of Sir John Lauder in 1900. His description of Oxford offers a fairly standard visit to several colleges – here he describes dining at Christ Church.

From that he led me to their kitchin; wheir ware 16 spits full of meat rosting (sometymes they have 7 when the Colledge is full). Then he took me up to the dining hall, a large roome with a great many tables all covered with clean napry. Heir we stayed a while; then the butler did come, from whom he got a flaggon of beir, some bread, apple tarts and fleck pies, [1] with which he entertained me wery courteously. Then came in a great many students, some calling for on thing and some for another. Their are a 102 students in this Colledge besydes Canons and others.

Samuel Pepys, 1668

Samuel Pepys (1633–1703) was at various times a navy administrator, MP and president of the Royal society, and of course is famous for his diary, kept from 1660 until 1669 (online at www.pepysdiary.com). His brief account of a trip to Oxford here focuses somewhat on his expenditure.

Tuesday 9th June

When come to Oxford, a very sweet place: paid our guide, 1*l.* 2*s.* 6*d.* … To dinner; and then out with my wife and people, and landlord: and to him that showed us the schools and library, 10*s.* to him that showed us All Souls' College, and Chichly's picture, 5*s.*

So to see Christ Church with my wife, I seeing several others very fine alone, with W. Hewer, before dinner, and did give the boy that went with me, 1*s.*

Strawberries, 1*s.* 2*d.*

Dinner and servants, 1*l.* 0*s.* 6*d.*

After come home from the schools, I out with the landlord to

Brazen-nose College; — to the butteries, and in the cellar find the hand of the Child of Hales, …

Thence with coach and people to Physic-garden, 1*s.*

So to Friar Bacon's study: I up and saw it, and give the man, 1*s.*

Bottle of sack for landlord, 2*s.*

Oxford mighty fine place; and well seated, and cheap entertainment.

Lorenzo Magalotti, 1669

Lorenzo Magalotti (1637–1712) was an Italian thinker, writer and diplomat. He accompanied Cosimo III de Medici, Grand Duke of Tuscany, on his Grand Tour of Europe, including visiting England in 1669 where they met figures such as Samuel Pepys, Robert Hooke and Robert Boyle (the latter sat by Magalotti's bedside when he fell ill in Oxford). Magalotti's journal was published in 1821 as *Travels of Cosmo the Third, grand duke of Tuscany, through England during the reign of King Charles the second.*

His highness arrived at Oxford at one in the morning, and alighted at lodgings prepared for him at the Angel Inn, having refused those which had been politely offered him in Christ-Church College, by Dr. Fell, Dean of that College, who is vice-chancellor and deputy for my Lord Gilbert Sheldon, Archbishop of Canterbury, Chancellor of the University....

Before he went out on the morning of the 14th [May], there came in public procession, to pay their respects to his highness, the vice-chancellor, with the professors, representing the body of the university, having previously assembled for that purpose in the church of St Mary, which is particularly appropriated to the academical ceremonies. They were preceded by six beadles, three of whom carried the golden maces, and three the silver ones; and close behind these came the vice-chancellor, accompanied by the heads of houses, professors and other members of the university, the greater part in scarlet gowns adapted to their respective degrees, and varying according to the faculty they professed ; so that the theologians had them lined in the inside with black velvet; the lawyers and physicians with red, each having on his head a square cap answering to the colour of the gown. The vice-chancellor complimented the serene prince in the name of the university, expressing the general joy at his arrival, and inviting him to the House of Convocation. His highness replied to this civility in language demonstrative of his respect and satisfaction. No sooner had the academicians departed, than the mayor and aldermen, drest in scarlet, with attendants, the same as in other cities, presented themselves to his highness, to welcome him, and to make an offer of whatever might be either useful or agreeable to him. In no respect inferior to their courtesy, was that of his highness, in assuring them how much he was gratified by their kind and respectful offers. As soon as the magistracy had departed, his highness, accompanied by the vice-chancellor and other professors, went to the College of St Mary Magdalen, which stands without the Eastern gate of the city. At the gate his highness was received by Dr. Pierce, the president, and conducted to see the church, and other things belonging to that magnificent building… In addition to the magnificence of the building, which is ornamented with stone decorations, and embellished with statues (amongst which the most esteemed are one of Mary Magdalen, and another of Bishop Wainfleet, the founder) it has to boast the pleasantness of its gardens, in which are walks and promenades, in the making of which neither expense nor labour has been spared, all enclosed within the walls of the college, which are bathed by the river Charwell. This stream, famous for the abundance and diversity of its fish, which joins the Isis in the neighbouring plains, and flows jointly with it into the Thames, affords, by the murmuring of its waters, no small gratification to the members of this college, who, including fellows, scholars, chaplains, choristers, inferior masters of arts, officers, and servants, exceed the number of one hundred and fifty, all being subordinate to the authority of a president. During the short space of time that his highness remained in the college, various Latin compositions were recited by the young students in his praise, and congratulating him on his arrival; but from the peculiarity of the pronunciation, the purport of them could not be sufficiently understood. From this college his highness went in his carriage to that of All-Souls, where he was met by Dr. James, the master, and many of the collegians, in their gowns, by one of whom his arrival was welcomed in a short congratulatory Latin oration. His highness, accompanied by the master and collegians, viewed the principal apartments of the college, which, in size and arrangement, are not inferior to any in Oxford…

His highness then proceeded to view Christ's College which is the largest and richest in Oxford. Dr. Fell, Dean and President of the same, with other members of the college, received and attended upon his highness, conducting him to the most remarkable apartments destined for the ordinary business and occurrences of the college, where different Latin compositions in prose were repeated to his highness by the scholars, expressive of their pleasure and acknowledgment. The whole edifice is of square stone, built according to the rules of the Gothic order, and comprehends two spacious courts…

… his highness went to St John the Baptist's College, where he was met and waited upon by Dr. Menor, president, and the members of the college.

In ascending the staircase, and whilst he was visiting the principal apartments, different epigrams were recited to his highness by certain of the collegians, who walked before and escorted him; and in the hall an oration was made in testimony of the respect which they entertained for his person, and the obligation under which they all felt themselves.

His highness viewed the library, and the gallery, which, except the cieling, possesses no ornament but a portrait, drawn with a pen, of King Charles I., which is shewn as a curiosity (his statue, with that of the queen, his wife, made of brass, stands over the gates in the second court), and noticed also the two gardens contained within the precincts of the college, of which the most curious is that which is raised, and has a view of the country situated to the north… Thence his highness returned to the inn, and dined as usual with the gentlemen of his train.

After dinner, the scholars, anticipating his highness's going out, waited for him, drawn up in parade-order on both sides of the streets through which he was to pass, beginning at his highness's lodgings, and ending at the House of Convocation, to which, as he was attended by the vice-chancellor and the other public professors, he chose to go on foot. In the hall, which was full of scholars, masters of arts, and the heads of the university, a seat was prepared on a large carpet for his highness, in the place of honor. Behind him, on the left hand, was the the vice-chancellor, in the stall appropriated to him. His highness was seated, whilst Dr. suet, professor of civil law, made him a public acknowledgment in Latin, in the name of the university, for his goodness in honoring it with his presence, and ended the ceremony by proposing the admission of several members to the degree of master of arts. To gratify the professors, who desired the honor of his highness's presence at their lectures, he went to hear the lecturer in geometry, John Wallis, who has the reputation of being the greatest arithmetician in Europe; the lecturer in anatomy, Paris ; and the lecturer in experimental philosophy, Thomas Willis, the most distinguished of all the learned men in the university. With the same retinue of the vice-chancellor and professors, in their doctors' gowns, he repaired to the theatre, a modern building, oval rather than perfectly round, erected by the present Archbishop of Canterbury, Chancellor of the University, and successor of the Duke of Clarendon. The architecture is mixed, that is, partly Doric, and partly Latin or composite, which is not only stronger and more graceful but also more showy; so that, being judiciously ornamented in all its parts, it has a most beautiful effect, and forces the spectator to acknowledge that the whole structure has been tastefully and regularly arranged both within and without; and what increases its beauty, is its being painted almost all over in fresco. This theatre is used for the disputations which are held by the public professors on the days appointed by the statutes of the university for each faculty; and the stalls in which they sit, according to their respective privileges and degrees, are judiciously and handsomely arranged round it for this purpose.

From the theatre his highness went to the public library of the university (for every college has its own private library for the service of its members). This building, which is of no very large size, is in the form of a T, with two shelves for books, one above the other. On the bottom shelf are distributed, in six rows, the books in folio; in three others, those in quarto; and on the upper one, to which you ascend by wooden steps ingeniously placed at the corners and in the middle, the books are distributed in the same number of rows, those in folio, in three, and those of different sizes in six, being separately arranged according to the subjects they treat of. Amongst these are the works of Selden, and the volumes of manuscripts which the predecessor of the present Archbishop of Canterbury presented to the library, about 2300, which are kept separately along with a great number of manuscripts in all the Oriental languages, and, for greater security, are fastened to the shelves with chains.

The members of this university have so great a value for their library, that they prefer it, both as to the number and rarity of its books, to that of the Vatican, persuading themselves that there is none in Europe to be compared with it: but, considering it dispassionately, it does not contain so numerous or such scarce books, as to deserve the praise of being the only library, or the most considerable one in the world, there being many others which are equal and even superior to it.

In the gallery of the library, there are many portraits of men illustrious for their learning hung round the walls. The medals, both ancient and modern, which are preserved there in great numbers, were shewn to his highness; they are kept separate, and classed in their proper places, according to their dates, without any confusion. His highness likewise saw the sword which was sent by Pope Leo X to King Henry VIII before the apostacy, along with the title of Defender of the Faith; and there was also shewn to him a liquor, which, placed on the finest marble, penetrates it by its subtleness, and works itself in as deep as about the thickness of a piaster. In the school of music, to which a lecturer was appointed, by Dr. William Heyther, for the purpose of teaching the theory of that art, his highness heard different pieces of music and cantatas. He went next to the Anatomical Theatre; and, except the skin of a man stuffed with tow, a human foot, from the end of one of whose toes was a horn growing out, and sundry animals and skeletons hung up against the wall, there was little to be seen that was curious.

Thence his highness went to the Botanical Garden, situated near the gate of the city leading to London, which, from the smallness of its size, irregularity, and bad cultivation scarcely deserves to be seen. By the keeper of the garden, an elderly man of a fine countenance, and a perfect botanist, the plants of the greatest rarity were shewn to the serene prince, being all noted down and described in a printed sheet of paper, which he presented to his highness, who, after this, returned home, and supped alone as usual.

Oxford, which, from its pleasant and delectable situation, has been already stated to be the capital city of the county of the same name, stands in a plain, encircled by woods, which clothe the hills that surround it on every side; amongst these run the two rivers Cherwell and Isis, which, branching out and dividing themselves into several streams, turn a great number of mills in the vicinity, bathing and supplying that very beautiful country with abundance of water… The private houses are built with more elegance than is usual in this kingdom, being for the most part of stone; but the public edifices exhibit a singular magnificence, being all of square stone…

The population is made to appear considerable by the scholars (upwards of three thousand) who dwell there continually, pursuing their studies; for, otherwise, the natives of the place are but few, the best part of the city being occupied by the buildings of the colleges, which, with their dependencies, are very large. Hence the great importance of Oxford consists in its University, which has rendered its name so eminently distinguished…

[Magalotti then gives the history of each of the colleges and halls.]

On the following morning (the 15th) at an early hour, the vice-chancellor, accompanied by the public professors and other collegians, came again to pay their respects to his highness, who received them with expressions of much esteem, and of, acknowledgment for the polite attention shewn to him; and in taking leave of them, he signified that he was on the point of departing from Oxford, on his return to London.

Celia Fiennes, c.1694

Celia Fiennes (1662–1741), daughter of a republican politician, was a ground-breaking traveller who was unusual for exploring much of England purely for the sake of it – as she put it, "to regain my health by variety and change of air and exercise". she made multiple excursions across the country on horseback between 1684 and c.1703, and compiled her notes into a memoir – extracts were first published in 1812 – the first full text (used here) was published as *Through England on a side saddle* in 1888. Her account is quite breathless but also notable for its fresh and vivid tone.

Oxford opens to view 2 mile off, its scituation is ffine on a Round hill Environ'd Round with hills adorn'd with Woods and Enclosures, yet not so neare as to annoy ye town which stands pleasant and Compact. There is a ffine Caus[wa]y for neare two mile by the Road for the schollars to walke on, ye Theater stands the highest of all and much in ye middle Encompass'd with ye severall Colledges and Churches and other Buildings whose towers and spires appeares very Well at a Distance; the streetes are very Cleane and well Pitched and pretty broad. The high streete is a very Noble one, soe Larg and of a Greate Length. In this is ye University Church Called st Maryes, which is very large and Lofty but Nothing very Curious in it. The Theater is a Noble Pile of building, its Paved with Black and White Marble, exceeding Large and Lofty, built Round and supported by its own architecture all stone, noe pillars to support it; itt has windows all round and full of Gallery's ffor the spectators as well as Disputants when ye acts are at Oxford. Over the Rooff of this Large Roome are as Large roomes with severall Divissions which are Used for the Drying the Printed sheetes of bookes, and this has Light in Ovalls which is quite Round the Theater and in the Middle is a large Cupelow or Lanthorne Whence your Eye has a very ffine view of ye whole town and Country; this is all supported on its own work. Under the theater is a roome w[hi]ch is ffitted for printing, where I printed My name severall tymes. The outside of ye theater there is a pavement and spikes of Iron in a Raile round with pillars of stone to secure it from the street. Just by it is a little building wch is full of Antiquityes wch have many Curiositys in it of Mettles, stones, Ambers, Gumms.

There is the picture of a Gentleman [that] was a Great benefactor to it being a travailer; the fframe of his picture is all wood carved very finely with all sorts of figures, Leaves, birds, beast and flowers. He gave them 2 ffine gold Meddals or silve gilt wth two ffine great Chaines of the same, one was all curious hollow worke wch were given him by some prince beyond the sea. There is a Cane which looks like a solid heavy thing but if you take it in yor hands its as light as a feather, there is a Dwarfe shoe and boote, there are several Loadstones, and it is pretty to see how ye steele Clings or follows it, hold it on the top att some distance the needles stand quite upright, hold it on either side it moves towards it as it rises and falls.

There are several good Colledges I saw most of [them]. Waddom hall is but little; in Trinity Colledge is a fine neate Chapple, new made, finely painted. Christ Church is ye largest

Colledge. The Courts large, ye buildings large and lofty; in one of the Courts is a tower new built for to hang the Mighty Tom, that bell is of a Large size, so great a Weight they were forced to have engines from London to raise it up to the tower. There is a fine ring of bells in ye Colledge st Magdalines, its just by the river, there is to Maudline Hall (which is a very large and good Cloyster) a very fine gravell walk, two or 3 may walke abreast, and Rows of trees on either side, and this is round a water wch Makes it very pleasant.

St Johns Colledge had fine gardens and walkes but I did but just look into it, so I did into kings, and queens Colledges, and severall of the rest I looked into, they are much alike in building but none so large as Christ Church Colledge. I was in New Colledge wch is very neate, but not large, the buildings good, Ye Chapple very fine; Ye Garden was new makeing, there is a large bason of water In the Middle there is little walkes and mazes and round mounts for the schollars to divert themselves.

In Corpus Christus Colledge wch is but small there I was entertained at supper and eate of their very good bread and beare which is remarkably the best anywhere Oxford Bread is.

The Physick garden afforded great diversion and pleasure, the variety of flowers and plants would have entertained one a week. The few remarkable things I tooke notice off was ye Aloes plant wch is like a great flag in shape, leaves and Coullour, and grows in the fform of an open Hartichoake and towards the bottom of each Leafe its very broad and thicke, In wch there are hollows or receptacles for ye Aloes. There is also ye sensible plant, take but a Leafe between finger and thumb and squeeze it and it immediately Curles up together as if pained and after some tyme opens abroad again, it looks in Coullour like a filbert Leafe but much narrower and long. There is also the humble plant that grows on a long slender stalke and do but strike it, it falls flatt on ye ground stalke and all, and after some tyme revives againe and stands up, but these are nice plants and are kept mostly under Glass's, ye aire being too rough for them. There is ye wormwood sage Called Mountaigne sage, its to all appearance like Comon sage only of yellower green, a narrow long Leafe full of ribbs; In yor Mouth the flavour is strong of Wormwood to the taste. The library is as large as 2 or 3 roomes but old and a little disreguarded except one part wch is parted from the rest, wansecoated and fitted up neate and painted which was done by King james ye second wn he designed Maudling Colledg for his priests A seminary. Here I met wth some of my relations who accompanyed me about to see some of the Colledges I had not seen before, st John's Colledge which is large and has a ffine Garden at one Entrance of it with Large Iron-gates Carved and Gilt; its built round two Courts: the Library is two walks, one out of the other the inner one has severall Anatomy's in Cases and some other Curiosity of shells, stone, bristol Diamonds, skins of ffish and beasts. Here they have the Great Curiosity Much spoken off King Charles the ffirsts Picture; Ye whole Lines of fface band and garment to the shoulders and armes and garter is all written hand and Containes the whole Comon prayer, itts very small the Character, but where a straight Line is you May read a word or two; there is another of Gustaus Adolphus whose portraiture is represented to the Eye in writeing alsoe and Contains his whole Life and prowess, there is alsoe the Lord's prayer and ten Commandments in the Compass of a Crown piece; there are also severall books all of writing on vellum Leaves, and one book written in ye Chinease Caractor on the Indian barks off trees; there is alsoe a Book of the Genealogies of the Kings since the Conquest to King Charles the second, with the severall Coates all Gilded very fresh till the two or three Last wch is pretended to be difficient from the art being Lost of Laying Gold so ffine on anything to polish it, but thats a great Mistake for that art is still in use in England, but the Excuse served the Negligence or ignorance of the workman; there was alsoe One book wth severall Cutts in it off ye Conception of Christ till his Ascension. There was alsoe a ffine prayer book or Mass book of Q. Marias, this was in the new part of the Library which was neately wanscoated and adorned. There is a ffine grove of trees and walks all walled round. Queens Colledge

Library is all new and a stately building Emulating that of Christ Church in Cambridge, it is not so large and stands on one range of Pillars of stone, the other ffront being all with statues in stone, in Nitches and Carved adornements and on the tops ffigures and statues. The stair-Case is pretty broad but not so ffinely wanscoated or Carved as that at Cambridge, the roomes is Lofty, but not so large, Well Wanscoated and there is good Carvings; its Mostly full of Books in the severall divisions and great Globes, its boarded Under foot, there is no ballcoany because the prospect is but to a dead wall, its very handsom.

Trinity Colledge Chapple which was not ffinish'd the Last tyme I was at Oxford but now it is a Beautifull Magnifficent structure. Its Lofty and Curiously painted -the Rooffe and sides ye history of Christ's ascention a very ffine Carving of thin white wood just Like that at Windsor it being the same hand. The whole Chappel is Wanscoated with Walnut tree and the fine sweet wood ye same yt ye Lord Oxfford brought over when high admiral of England, and has wanscoated his hall and staircase with. It is sweet like Cedar and of a Reddish Coullr, but ye graine much ffiner and well vein'd.

New Colledge which belongs to the ffiennes's, William of Wickam the founder, so I look'd on myself as some way a little Interested in that, here I was very handsomly Entertained by Mr Cross wch was one of my nephew say and seale's Tutors when at Oxfford. These ffellowshipp in New Colledge are about 100 say and a very pretty appartinent of Dineing Roome, bed Chamber, a studdy and a room for a servant, tho' ye serviteurs of the Colledge gives attendance; and here they may Live very Neatly and well if sober and have all their Curiosityes they take much delight in, greens of all sorts, Myrtle, oringe and Lemons and Lorrestine growing in potts of Earth and so moved about from place to place and into the aire sometymes. There are severall New Lodgings added and beautifyed here, the Gardens also wth gravell and Grass walkes, some shady and a great mount in the Middle wch is ascended by Degrees in a round of Green paths deffended by greens cutt Low, and on ye top is a summer house.

Beyond these Gardens is a bowling-green and round it a Close shady walke, walled round and a Cutt hedge to the bowling-green.

There are in Oxford 18 Colledges and six halls *[a list follows]*… There is a very odd Custom In Queen Coll. for every new-years-day, there is a Certain sum Laid out In Needles and thread wch was Left by ye founder and every Gentleman of that Colledge has one given him wth these words: *Take this and be thrifty.*

In New Colledge Garden in ye plott there is ye Colledg Armes Cutt in box and ye 24 Letters round it. Next plott a sun-dial cutt in box and true-Lovers knotts; att ye entrance Of ye Colledge over ye gate is the ffiennes's and ye Wickhams Arms Cutt in stone sett up there by my Nephew say when he was at ye Colledge before his travels. There is a large stone statue in the Middle of ye first quadrangle of William of Wickhams ye ffounder, railed in wth Iron Grates. In ye Library are ye pictures of some of ye learned men wch belonged formerly to the University.

Francis Burman, 1702

Francis Burman (1671–1719) was a Dutch pastor who had studied at the University of Leyden; his father was Professor or Divinity at Utrecht. Burman junior accompanied a group of his fellow Dutchmen on a trip to England – his diary, published in English in 1911,[1] is somewhat brief and matter-of-fact.

24 *July, Monday*. Set out for *Oxford*: put up at the *Cross*.

25 *July, a.m.* Degrees conferred, *p.m.* saw *New college*, 'admodum augustum.'

26 *July, p.m.* Saw the *Bodleian*; climbed *Ch[rist] Ch[urch]* tower.

27 *July, a.m.* Walked to a mineral spring in the neighbourhood. *p.m.* Heard the exercises in the *Sheldonian* theatre. saw the laboratory.

Saw *Trinity college*. Then in the house of convocation at the election of two members of parliament. Then Dr. *Hudson* took me to the *Bodleian*, to the library of *Qu[een's] coll.*, and to Dr. *Mill* in St *Edm[und] hall…*

p.m. After the departure of my dutch friends, I began to examine the library, especially the MSS. of the N.T.

29 *July a.m.* and *p.m.* in the Bodleian.

30 *July, a.m.* saw the university church St Mary's, 'satis augustum.' Heard [bishop] *Hall's* sermon in his parish church, where he preaches weekly. Was then at a quakers' meeting. *p.m.* At prayers in a suburban church; also in the fine chapel of *New college*. Then saw *Magd. coll.* walks.

31 *July, a.m.* in the *Bodleian. p.m.* saw St *Jo. Bapt. coll.* with its fine library, of books and Mss.; *Balliol, University, All Souls'.*

1 *Aug. a.m.* In the library. *p.m.* Rode to Woodstock.

2 *Aug. a.m.* and *p.m.* In the library. With Mr. *Gregory* visited the most famous *[John] Wallis*, a man of astonishing vigour for his age. He is 86, and yet reads very readily without spectacles, which he has never used; rises at five daily; studies, for more than 10 hours, mathematics amongst other things; is equally strong in judgement and in memory, neither of which is in the least impaired. His face is cheerful and open…

3 *Aug. a.m.* in the library. saw the *hortus medicus*. Quaintly trimmed yews. p.m. In the library.

---

1. In *Cambridge under Queen Anne*, edited by J.E.B. Mayor.

John Dunton, 1704

John Dunton (1659–1733) was a bookseller and author, and creator of England's first major periodical, The Athenian Mercury. He travelled to America, Holland and Ireland, writing of some of his travels in letters and journals. His pamphlet *A Step to Oxford in which is comprehended An Impartial Account of the University* was published in 1704; his criticisms of the colleges are not particularly 'impartial' but his account of his arrival with a 'young gentleman' and his two sisters is much less acerbic.

Judging our London atmosphere grosser, more implete and pregnant with infectious and distempering Exhalations than that of the Country, and being highly nauseated with the foetid emanations of putrefied Carcasses: I thought it extremely necessary for my own Preservation, to visit the Rural, Flowry, & Delightsome Plains. Having not as yet determin'd which way I should steer my Course, at last I resolv'd for Oxon… Accordingly on the 26 of May, a Young Gentleman with two Young Ladies and my self took Coach about Seven a Clock in the Morning…

We were now to my great satisfaction come to Oxford: Having not as yet resolv'd on any particular Lodging: I recommended to the young Gentleman the Angel in Broad-street which we accordingly took for our lodgings. Being somewhat fatigu'd by our Journy, we order'd our Landlady to get Supper ready, as soon as possible; in half an hour it was brought on the Table… As soon as had Sup'd, the next thing enquir'd after was our Beds, we were told that these were provided for us…

The Weather being mighty Clear and Serene they were very earnest to refresh themselves with a Pleasant Walk. I tender'd my service, and promis'd to show them the finest Walk as 'tis reported in the whole Kingdom… I granted their Request, and accordingly show'd them to Maudlin-walks. The young Gentleman said that he thought they were adorn'd with all things requisite to render them extremely Delightsome. He protested that he never saw more exact position and order of Trees Rivetted thro'out the whole Walk. That he never beheld a more Verdant and Flowry Meadow; he extoll'd the contrivance of the Ground, its easy Ascents and Degradations, its Smoothness, its well Proportion'd Latitude and Moderate Length. The Pleasure occasion'd by the Murmuring noise of the Adjacent River he thought extremely Ravishing, and Delightsome. To see the Fishes besporting themselves in their proper Element, Decoy'd and Caught by the vigilant and dextrous Angler was accounted by him pleasant Interruptions and Diverting delays in Walking.

Having Recreated our selves, we return'd to our Lodgings; Dinner was immediately brought to Table; as soon as we had Din'd, we went to see the Theatre, and Laboratory. There were a vast number of Rarities worthy of Observation; of which you might expect a particular Account, did not brevity of time prevent me.

Having spent the Day to satisfie my Companys Curiosity, I thought it necessary for my own Refreshment to revive by Drooping Spirit with an enlivening Bottle. I ask'd the young Gentleman to go with me, who very willingly accepted my offer;

We went to the King's-head, w[h]ere the Wine was so intolerably Sophisticated that we were constrain'd to depart sooner than we first design'd. Ale is the Prime Commodity that is here afforded, 'tis in it our Gownsmen liquidate their Coin…

Ludvig Holberg, 1706

Ludvig Holberg (1684–1754) was a major figure in Norwegian literature, best known for his comic plays. The Memoirs of Lewis Holberg were published in 1737, and then in English in 1827; they include an account of his time staying in Oxford.

We lived three months at Oxford with so rigid an attention to economy, that we eat meat only once in four days; on the other three days we were obliged to be contented with bread and cheese, or even a more scanty and unsubstantial repast. My health and strength, to which a frugal mode of living has always been favourable, continued unimpaired; but my companion, who had not been accustomed to such meagre diet, lost his strength and flesh rapidly. Whenever the cravings of his stomach reminded him of his misfortunes, he cursed our ill-advised journey, and above all deplored the loss of the money which we had so improvidently thrown away for the sake of obtaining access to the library. At length he became melancholy, and wished to avoid altogether the society of mankind. I endeavoured to rally his spirits, by quoting among other things the facetious observation of Bion, that it is absurd to tear our hair when we are in affliction, as if baldness were a remedy for sorrow. But I was addressing a man whom grief had rendered insensible, and on whom neither exhortation nor raillery could make the slightest impression.

[They visit a banker in London to revive their finances.]

… on our return to Oxford we indulged freely in the pleasures of a tavern which was much frequented by the students, with many of whom we soon became acquainted. There was a Scotchman, however, who, though he had formerly cultivated our society, received us coldly from the time we began to frequent the tavern. We were ignorant of the cause of this alteration in his conduct, until he told us, that he considered it highly indecorous in students to frequent taverns, and that at any rate it was very unusual to indulge in such excesses at Oxford. It is undoubtedly true, that there is scarcely any institution for public instruction in which the authorities are more respected, and in which the conduct of the students is more uniformly correct and decorous, than the university of Oxford. Here the most trivial offences are noticed and corrected: and the benefit which the students derive from this salutary discipline, is as striking as is the mischief which results from an opposite system in some other seats of learning, which are at the same time schools for drinking, feasting, gaming, and every species of debauchery. If you go out after ten o'clock at Oxford, it is difficult to imagine that you are in the midst of a populous city, so complete is the solitude, so profound the silence which reigns around you.

In the evening, censors chosen annually, called proctors, visit all parts of the city; and if any students are discovered in taverns, or other improper haunts, they are subject to heavy fines and impositions. It is ridiculous enough, however, that these moral regulations do not extend to those who are distinguished by the higher academical degrees; for doctors and masters of arts enjoy the right of drinking in taverns till daybreak, and the attainment of the superior degrees confers the twofold privilege of disputing and of carousing in public. Hence the votaries of Bacchus have a strong motive for aspiring to honours to which such advantages are annexed; and there can be little doubt, that if the same encouragement were held out to students in other universities, the cause of philosophy would be greatly advanced.

It is said, indeed, that this ingenious distinction is founded upon the supposition, that men who are distinguished by academical honours would spontaneously abstain from vices which others can only be deterred from committing by the fear of punishment. Certain it is, however, that most of the carousals and drinking-bouts in taverns take place under the auspices of masters of arts. I remember the students were often caught in our tavern; but whenever a superior graduate was present, they boldly told the proctors that they were in the company of masters of arts; upon which the censors immediately retired. If this little work admitted of such details, could enter into many amusing particulars respecting this university; but I design I only to present my readers with a short, simple narrative of my life, and to that object I shall endeavour to confine myself.

… I remained at Oxford, after the departure of Brixius, about fifteen months, during all which time lived in gay and sumptuous style; being invited almost every day by the fellows of colleges to dine and sup, or, as they say at Oxford, to take commons with them. For a long time was known to the Oxonians by no other name than *Myn Heer*, that designation having, in the first instance, been given to me and my companion by our barber, who took us for Germans, and was desirous of showing that he was not altogether ignorant of our language, though he knew nothing beyond those two words. *Myn Heer* was so often repeated by the barber, that it was caught up by others; and as I did not care to correct the mistake, I should probably have been known at Oxford by no other appellation, if I had not accidentally met with a student of the name of Holberg, to whom I communicated the fact of our having the same name. As, in addition to this coincidence of names, his manners and pursuits agreed with mine, a friendship was soon formed between us, and I used sometimes to tell him playfully, that we probably came from the same stock, and were lineally descended from one of my ancestors who came over to Britain with Canute the Great.

William Stukeley, 1710

William Stukeley (1687–1765) is one of Britain's most notable antiquarians, and is particularly known for his studies of Stonehenge and Avebury. He was also a clergyman and physician. Between 1710 and 1725 he took many journeys on horseback to investigate ancient sites across England. His 1710 *Iter Oxoniense*, excerpted here, describes a journey from Lincolnshire to Oxfordshire.

Oxford requires a more elaborate description than a stranger can possibly give; and indeed so numerous are the colleges and halls, that one can scarce get a tolerable idea of them in the three days I staid here. The prospect of this place from Shotover hill is very inviting, nor is our expectation frustrated when in the place. The bridge over the Cherwel is a stately work, twice as broad as London bridge. Magdalen college, the legacy of our countryman, William of Wainflet, which he endowed with a princely hand, deservedly is thought one of the noblest foundations in Europe: the old oak is still left, nigh which he ordered it to be built. A vast tract of ground is inclosed with a castellated wall for gardens. On the other fide the river is a park too, with long shady walks, but too near the water, wherein likewise more resembling those of Academus by Athens. The chapel is large and magnificent: the tower is a lofty strong work, in it a fine ring of bells: the whimsical figures in the quadrangle, over the buttresses, amuse the vulgar; they are the licentious inventions of the mason. Over-against this is the physic garden, whose curiosities Mr. Bobart showed us, and his own: since his death, its purpose is not so well executed. Here are remarkably fine greens in all the gardens at Oxford, especially in yew: the two piers here, with flower-pots on them, are thought to exceed; but the two yew men (as one waggishly called them) that guard the door, are ridiculous; the architecture of these gates is, I suppose, of Inigo Jones: two *sphynges* at the entrance are properly placed: these are without the city walls.

University college has a new quadrangle built by legacy of Dr. Radcliffe; but I think uniformity, in this and other structures in the university, no sufficient reason for using the old manner of building. Queen's college over-against it is of a good taste, improved to its present splendor under the auspices, and in great degree at the charge, of the late Dr. Lancaster. The library, the hall, and chapel, are beautiful. The old gatehouse has a pretty cieling over it of stone; they fay it was the chamber of Harry the Vth's uncle and tutor. Behind it is New college; a large chapel, a good visto to the garden, in which is a pleasant mount: this was the foundation of William of Wickham, bishop of Winchester: it stands in an angle of the old city walls. At All souls a new court is building, but in the anachronism of the Gothic degenerate taste: the new library is a spacious room, the legacy of colonel Coddrington: the chapel is very elegant; the altar, entirely of marble, was made at the charge of George Clark, esq. one of the fellows.

Christ church, the magnificent work of cardinal Wolsey: the stone cieling over the entrance to the hall is very pretty; the new quadrangle, designed by the learned Dr. Aldrich, is beautiful. St John's college has two handsome quadrangles, the portico's built by archbishop Laud: two fine statues, in brass, of king Charles I. and his queen, probably designed by Inigo Jones.

But it is impossible for me to run through the whole of this splendid university, which I leave as a fitter task for some of her own learned sons. The school is a large building: the Bodleian library, an immense store-house of most valuable books and manuscripts, the donation of archbishop Laud, the earl of Pembroke, O. Cromwell, Selden, Digby, Bodley, and other great names over it is a spacious gallery, adorned with pictures of founders, benefactors, and others, and with the antique marbles which were the learned part of the inexhaustible collection of the earl of Arundel: these have been illustrated with the accurate comments of Selden and Prideaux. Here are some of the most valuable Greek monuments now in the world. Over the porch, upon a handsome pedestal of black marble, stands the brass effigies of the earl of Pembroke, their noble and generous chancellor, given by the present earl: this was moulded by Rubens. Here is likewise a very large collection of Greek, Roman, British, Saxon, English, and other coins, presented by several hands. The divinity schools, finished by Humphry the good duke of Gloucester, has a very curious ston[e] roof.

The Ashmolean repository, beside some good books, papers and Mss. of the founder, has a large collection of rarities in antiquity, nature and art, &c. such as original pictures of famous men, marbles of old Egyptian carving in figures and hieroglyphics, a fine marble inscription in Arabic, which was over the door of a school at Tangier; an Egyptian mummy, being a man dressed like *orus Apollo*; the cradle of Henry VI. the hat of Bradshaw plaited with steel within, under which he sat in judgment upon king Charles J. a vast fund of precious and other stones, &c. which it is impossible to enumerate. Here is, beside, a choice apparatus of instruments for chymistry and experimental philosophy under the direction of Mr. Whiteside. The printing-house is a good building with a bold portico, but next the schools disgraced with a wretched statue of my lord Clarendon.

Between these two last and the schools stands the Sheldonian theatre, the first piece of architecture of sir Christopher Wren, a spacious and well-proportioned room: it is worth while to go upon the top of it, to see the carpentry of the roof, and the fine prospect of the city and country thence.

Before Baliol college they showed us the stone in the street which marks the place of the barbarous martyrdom of the venerable archbishop Cranmer and bishop Ridley, then upon the banks of the ditch without the walls of the city, which went along where the theatre now stands.

Beyond the river, amongst meadows encompassed with rivulets, stood Oseney abbey, founded by Robert D'oyley 1129. Upon the bridge is a tower called Friar Bacon's study, from that famous and learned monk, who in dark ages had penetrated so far into the secrets of nature. Oxford, no doubt, means no more than the passage over the river Ox, Ouse, or Isis, which are equivalents. Over another bridge of the Isis we went to see Ruleigh abbey, where some ruins and parcels still remain, turned to a common brew-house: a disjointed stone in a partition wall preserves [a] monumental inscription…

Of the castle there is a square high tower remaining by the river side, and a lofty mount or keep walled at top, with a staircase going downward: this seems to have been a very strong place, built by Robert de Oili in the time of William the Conqueror. If there was a town here in Roman times, it seems to have been in this quarter. The White-friars was a royal palace; and near a green called Beaumonds, they showed us the bottom of a tower upon the ground where the valiant Richard I. Coeur de lion was born.

Without the town on all sides may be seen the remains of the fortifications raised in the time of the civil wars. It is in vain to pretend in this paper to enumerate the particular remarkables of every college, which are eighteen in number, and seven halls: these for beauty, grandeur, and endowment, no doubt exceed any thing: their chapels, halls, libraries, quadrangles, piazzas their gardens, walks, groves, and every thing, contribute to make the first university in the world. As to the city, though the colleges make up two thirds of it, and are continually eating it away, in buying whole streets for enlargement, yet it is large, regular, and crouds itself out proportionably: the streets are spacious, handsome, clean, and strait; the whole place pleasant and healthful; the inhabitants genteel and courteous: the churches are many and elegant enough, especially Allhallows, a neat fabric of modern architecture, with a very handsome spire. St Peter's in the east is venerable for its antiquity: the east end by its fabric appears prior to the time of the Conquest.

Leaving this famous repository of learning, we saw on our left hand, on the other fide of the river, the last ruins of Godstow nunnery, placed among the sweet meadows: here fair Rosamond, the beloved mistress of Henry II. had a tomb remarkably fine; but before the dissolution, scarce could her ashes rest, whose beauty was thought guilty even after death.

Zacharias von Uffenbach, 1710

Zacharias Conrad von Uffenbach (1683–1734) was a German scholar and bibliophile who kept an extensive journal of his 1710 visit to England. He wrote of the library collections of London, Oxford and Cambridge in extensive detail, along with observations of English social life, often giving his own strong opinions. The extracts here are from W.H. Quarrell's 1928 translation, *Oxford in 1710.*

In the afternoon of 17 August, we wandered about to see the town generally, and found it rather better than Cambridge, though were it not for the more important colleges, the place would be not unlike a large village. As among other places we passed the Physic Garden or *Hortus Medicus* we entered to have a look at it. It is opposite Magdalen College, not very large, and fairly well laid out, but it is ill-kept and everything in the flower-beds appeared wild and over-grown. The large yews provide the chief ornament; I have nowhere met with finer or better-trained specimens than here. One finds many different figures made out of them, and two especially; of unheard-of size just at the entrance gates are exceptionally fine trees cut with shears to represent, one Hercules with the club, the other a man with a spear. Both are about thirty feet high. Finally there are two pilasters of the same work each with a vase of flowers artistically cut and very pretty.

At Magdalen College we saw the chapel, which is very elegant but small and rather dark. At the entrance to the chapel, we found various epitaphs to men of learning, which I need not copy, as they are quoted by Wood in his History and Antiquities of Oxford.

On 18 August, Monday morning, our first care was to view the world-famed public library of this University, or the Bodleian, as it is commonly called, after its founder, and to make ourselves known to the Librarian. We asked him to let us have a pass; for unless this is in order, no book may be touched and one sees nothing except what the assistant librarians choose to show for an honorarium, only too often all sorts of rubbish little likely to please anyone who is in search of something more profound. But as it costs about eight shillings and some trouble to gain an entrance, most strangers content themselves with a casual inspection. Every moment brings fresh spectators of this description and, surprisingly enough, amongst them peasants and womenfolk, who gaze at the library as a cow might gaze at a new gate with such a noise and trampling of feet that others are much disturbed. So that we might not proceed likewise, we begged the *Proto-Bibliothecarius*, Dr. Hudson, to procure us a pass, which he readily gave. We supposed that this happened out of courtesy, but learned later it was rather from cupidity and in anticipation of getting large donations out of us.

To get ourselves into the good graces of Master Crab, the Sub-Librarian, a poor covetous man, and to take the opportunity of giving him his customary gratuity of a crown, we asked him to guide us round, principally to see the arrangement of the library in general...

. . .

22 August was spent in the Bodleian Library. On 23 August we wished to go to the Ashmolean Museum; but it was market day and all sorts of country-folk, men and women, were up there for the leges that hang up on the door *parum honeste & liberaliter* allow everyone to go in. 50, as we could have seen nothing well for the crowd, we went down-stairs again and saved it for another day…

In the afternoon of 16 September a race meeting was held about a mile and a half away from the City. This happens every year in Oxfordshire. We took a boat up the Thames, which flows past the fields in which the races are held. This meadow is two and a half miles in circumference and much more suited for a race-course than the one at Epsom, though it is somewhat marshy. Many booths had been set up, where beer was sold, each of which had its sign, a hat, a glove and suchlike. Nearly all the people from the town were there and also many strangers, some riding, some driving, some in boats.

The horses which were to run were six in number and had to race twice round the whole course—five English miles, which took inside ten minutes. A horse belonging to the Duke of Beaufort won two successive races; in the second race another horse would have passed him, but jumped over a woman, who had got in his way, and thus wrenched his leg. It is incredible what jumps these horses make and how fast they run…

On the morning of 17 September we were in the library. The Librarian Dr. Hudson looked through with us the books which we had selected from the duplicates, and quoted the price, which was so high that my brother only kept a few mathematical books. I was not a little annoyed that he often asked ten shillings for a book which he afterwards parted with for five or six. I hear he is said to be very self-seeking and to have earned large sums with his book peddling: but he has made many enemies through his greed and is generally called the "Bookseller." His erudition is not very much thought of nor did I detect much of it in my intercourse with him. To all appearance he is very affable, but he has a very disagreeable habit, when he is talking, of crying out every moment: "He! he! he!" just like the peasants, so that it can be heard through the whole library. He is not particularly industrious in the library and the two Sub-Librarians, Mr. Crab, but in particular Mr. Hearne, have made the new catalogue. This Hearne is a man of thirty, very inconspicuous, but a hard worker and of considerable learning… *[See the next chapter for Hearne himself.]*

On 19 September… [we] went to the *Hortus Medicus* with Dr. Buttner, who had just arrived a few days before. He had introductions from London to Professor Bobart, and as he was a great lover of botany and a connoiseur, I considered it advisable that we should see the garden straightway in his company, so as the sooner and the better to profit by it.

As we were going out, we met a funeral, and I must mention this before I speak of the garden, as it was so curious. The coffin, over which was spread a large black velvet pall, stood on two chairs before the door of a house. When the time came to make a move, some wretched fellows in coloured clothing crept under the cloth and took the coffin on their shoulders without a bier. About eight respectable townsfolk (who however like all those accompanying the body, with the exception of the mourners and relations, were not in black) seized the corners of the velvet pall and carried them, and after them followed about eight couples of mourners or relatives, male and female, who walked two and two leaving the others to follow in a crowd. As I have said, they all marched along in colours and every one had a stick of rosemary in one hand and in the other a white roll of paper containing white gloves. The house of mourning provides both of these a great expense, as the poorest quality cost at least one shilling and sixpence. Distinguished people are buried by torchlight.

We entered the *Hortus Medicus [i.e. the Physic Garden]* and Professor Bobart was waiting for us. I was greatly shocked by the hideous features and generally villainous appearance of this good and honest man. His wife, a filthy old hag, was with him, and although she may be the ugliest of her sex he is certainly the more repulsive of the two. An unusually pointed and very long nose, little eyes set deep in the head, a twisted mouth almost without upper lip, a great deep scar in one cheek and the whole face and hands as black and coarse as those of the poorest gardener or farm-labourer. His clothing and especially his hat were also very bad. Such is the aspect of the Professor, who would most naturally be taken for the gardener. In point of fact he does nothing else but work continually in the garden, and in the science of botany he is the careful gardener rather than the learned expert. Yet the industry of the man in publishing the works of his predecessor Morison, who far excelled him in learning, is as praiseworthy as his work in the garden. To come to the garden itself, the good man conducted us round most willingly and showed us all he had, a considerable number of items, but not approaching in interest either those in Leyden or in Amsterdam.

John Macky, 1714

John Macky (d.1726) was a Scottish spy and the first to report on the exiled James II's intended invasion of England in 1692. Macky also wrote a journal of travels across Scotland, and *A journey through England in familiar letters from a gentleman here to his friend abroad*, published in 1714.

Oxford makes by much the best outward Appearance of any City I have seen, being visible for several Miles round on all sides, in a most delightful Plain; and adorned with the steeples of the several Colleges and Churches, which make a glorious show.

[The colleges and their history are listed, as well as the usual sites of interest. More unusual are the details of the Bodleian Library that follow.]

THE Library-Keeper is elected and admitted to his Office, after the same Manner as the Proctors are chosen and admitted to their Office, by delivering the Keys of the Library into his Custody; only the Candidates must submit themselves to the Examinations of the Curators: Both the Electors and the Person elected, must take the proper Oaths directed in the Bodleian statutes. This Library is open on all Days of the Year, besides Sundays, Christmas Day, and Holydays, from Eight a-Clock in the Morning to Eleven, and from Two in the Afternoon to Five, from Easter to Michaelmas and the other Part of the Year, from One till Four a-Clock, unless on Saturdays, when it is only open till Three a Clock in the Afternoon, for the sake of cleaning it. Neither the Librarian, nor his Deputy, may on any Pretence whatsoever, carry in any Candle or Fire, on Pain of perpetual Amotion; and the Keeper ought not to be absent from thence, above a Day and a half, on Pain of 20 shillings to be lopped off from his salary, for the Increase of Books.

Thomas Hearne, 1715-29

Thomas Hearne (1678–1735) was an antiquarian and prolific diarist. After attending Oxford University, he became assistant keeper at the Bodleian Library until he was, in his words "locked out of the library" in 1716 (for refusing an oath of allegiance to George I). He remained in Oxford and provides many rich accounts of the city's history and social life. Below are just a few selections on particular events and local customs, from *The Remains of Thomas Hearne*, published in 1869.

1715

May 29. Last night a good part of the presbyterian meeting-house in Oxford was pulled down. There was such a concourse of people going up and down, and putting a stop to the least sign of rejoycing, as can not be described. But then the rejoicing this day (notwithstanding Sunday) was so very great and publick in Oxford, as hath not been known hardly since the restauration. There was not an house next the street but was illuminated. For if any disrespect was shewn, the windows were certainly broke. The people run up and down, crying *King James the third! The true king! No usurper! The duke of Ormond!* &c. and healths were every where drank suitable to the occasion, and every one at the same time drank to a new restauration, which I heartily wish may speedily happen.

In the evening they pulled a good part of the quakers' and anabaptists' meeting houses down. This rejoicing hath caused great consternation at court. The heads of houses have represented that it was begun by the whiggs, who met at the King's Head Tavern on Saturday night, under the denomination of the constitution club , and being about to carry on extravagant designs, they were prevented by an honest party that were in an adjoyning room, and forced to sneak away. Some of these fanatical persons shot off guns in some places, and had like to have killed many. Two or three were wounded…

June 5. King George being informed of the proceedings of the cavaliers at Oxford, on Saturday and Sunday, (May 28, 29,) he is very angry, and by his order, Townshend, one of the secretaries of state, hath sent rattling letters to Dr. Charlett, pro-vice-chancellor, and the mayor. Dr. Charlett shewed me his this morning. This lord Townshend says, his majesty (for so they will stile this silly usurper) hath been fully assured that the riots both nights were began by scholars, and that scholars promoted them, and that he (Dr. Charlett) was so far from discountenancing them, that he did not endeavour in the least to suppress them. He likewise observes, that his majesty was as well informed that the other magistrates were not less remiss on these occasions. The heads have had several meetings upon this affair, and they have drawn up a *programma*, (for they are obliged to do something,) to prevent the like hereafter; and this morning very early, old Sherwin the yeoman beadle was sent to London to represent the truth of the matter.

. . .

August 17. When king Charles II entered London, on the 29th of May, upon his restoration, it was a most lovely fine day, and there was a prodigious number of people that flocked to see the entrance from all parts. The king rid upon an horse, and as he passed along he was very complaisant and pleasant to all people, and pulled off his hat to all, but especially to the ladies, to whom he bowed in a very courteous manner, shewing a particular regard to that sex, which gained him much esteem likewise from them.

1721

Sept 6. In the year 1702 Queen Anne was at Oxford, lay at Christ Church, and the next day dined in the theater with prince George, (her husband,) the duke and dutchess of Marlborough, &c.; Dr. Maunder was vice-chancellor. She was very merry, and eat most heartily. After dinner she passed through the Ashmolean Museum, took coach, and so went out of town for the Bath. Humphrey Wanley was at the same time in Oxford, as I well remember, and then wore a long wig, (tho now he wears his own hair,) and strutted mightily about. This Wanley hath reported since he hath been now in Oxford, (a thing I had not heard of before,) that he was sent for at that time on purpose to shew the queen the curiosities of the Bod- leian Library, had she went up thither, as she did not. Thus this vain coxcombe.

1723

Feb. 27. It hath been an old custom in Oxford for the scholars of all houses, on Shrove Tuesday, to go to dinner at ten clock, (at which time the little bell, called pan-cake bell, rings, or at least should ring, at St Maries,) and at four in the afternoon ; and it was always followed in Edmund hall, as long as I have been in Oxford, till yesterday, when they went to dinner at twelve, and to supper at six, nor were there any fritters at dinner, as there used always to be. When laudable old customs alter, 'tis a sign learning dwindles.

Sept 5. Yesterday, at two clock in the afternoon, was a smoaking match over against the Theater in Oxford, a scaffold being built up for it just at Finmore's, an alehouse. The conditions were, that any one (man or woman) that could smoak out three ounces of tobacco first, without drinking or going off the stage, should have twelve shillings. Many tryed, and 'twas thought that a journyman taylour, of St Peters in the East, would have been victor, he smoaking faster than, and being many pipes before, the rest; but at last he was so sick, that 'twas thought he would have dyed; and an old man, that had been a souldier, and smoaked gently, came off conquerour, smoaking the three ounces quite out, and he told one, (from whom I had it,) that, after it, he smoaked four or five pipes the same evening.

1725

Jan. 19. They have a custom in St Aldgate's parish, Oxford, for people of the parish to eat sugar sopps out of the font in the church, every holy Thursday, and this is done in the morning.

1729

Dec. 31. On Monday last was to have been a prize fighting in Oxford between two fellows, and they had it cryed about with beat of drum for some time the mayor, Sir Oliver Greenaway having given them leave: but they having had no leave from the Vice-Chancellour, the same was stopt, the Vice-Chancellour taking one of them up a little before the time of fighting, and laying in wait yesterday for the other, or any one else that was to abett and countenance such a proceeding, to the great Resentment of Some townsmen, who aim at destroying the Privileges of the University, one of which is to prevent and obstruct all idle, vagrant, dissolute persons who carry arms to the disturbance of the publick peace, and of the Discipline of the University.

Nicholas Amhurst, 1721

Nicholas Amhurst (1697–1742) was a poet and political writer who attended St John's College, Oxford, but was expelled in 1719. Two years later he used the pseudonym Terrae Filius to pen a series of satirical letters about life in the city and its university, published in 1726 as *Terræ-filius: or, the Secret History of the University of Oxford.*

[Amhurst begins by explaining the name he has adopted.]

It has, till of late, been a custom, from time immemorial, for one of our family to mount the *Rostrum* at *Oxford* at certain seasons, and divert innumerable crowd of spectators, who flock'd thither to hear him from all parts, with a merry oration in the *Fescennine* manner, interspers'd with secret history, raillery, and sarcasm, as the occasions of the times supply'd him with matter.

If a venerable Head of a college was caught snug a-bed with his neighbour's wife; or shaking his elbows on a *Sunday* morning; or flattering a prime minister for a bishoprick; or coaxing his bed-maker's girl out of her maidenhead; the boary old sinner might expect to hear of it from our lay-pulpit the next *Act.* Or if a celebrated *toast* and a young student were seen together at midnight under a shady myrtle-tree, billing like two pretty turtle-doves, to *him* it belong'd, being a poet as well as an orator, to tell the tender story in a melancholy ditty, adapted to pastoral musick.

Wednesday, February 22

Of all the sumptuous *Edifices* which of late years have shot up in Oxford, and adorned the habitation of the muses, the new *Printing-house*, commonly called Clarendon's *Printing-house*, strikes me with particular pleasure and veneration: it is, I do assure my reader, a most magnificent and stately pile of building, suitable to those great ends for which it was raised. This is the *midwife* in ordinary to *Alma Mater*, which delivers the profound genius's of the university of all those voluminous offsprings, to which the common wealth of letters is so much indebted and obliged.

Concerning the origination of this useful fabrick, divers rumours are gone forth; some say, the money, which was appropriated for this end, being *embezzel'd*, it was carried on at the charge of the university treasury: others, that *certain books* were sold for the fourth part of the prime cost, to defray this expence; which procedure was, I suppose, founded upon this politick supposition, that when they had got a new *Printing-house*, they could never want new *books*; but by what means soever it was built, my lord Clarendon has the honour, and we, his happy posterity, the invaluable benefit of it…

But Printing is not the only, nor the principal use, for which these stupendous stone-walls were erected; for here is that famous apartment, by idle wits and buffoons nick-named Golgotha, *i.e.* the place of Sculls or Heads of colleges and halls, where *they* meet and debate upon all extraordinary affairs, which occur within the precincts of their jurisdiction. This *room* of *state*, or academical *council-chamber* is adorn'd with a fine pourtrait of her late majesty Queen ANNE, which was presented to this assembly by a jolly *fox-hunter* in the neighbourhood, out of the tender regard which he bore to her pious memory, and to the reverend Sculls of the university, who preside there; for which benefaction they have admitted him into their company, and allow him the honour to smoak a pipe with them *twice a week.*

This Room is also handsomely *wainscotted*; which is said to have been done by order of a certain worthy gentleman, who went to *Oxford* for a Degree without any claim or recommendation; and therefore, to supply that defect, promised to become a *benefactor*, if they would make him a *graduate*; accordingly, as it is said, workmen were employed in great haste, and the Sculls, lest they should be behind hand in gratitude, in as great haste, clapp'd a Degree upon his back; but the story unfortunately concludes, that when the Graduate was created, the *benefactor* ran away, and left the good-natur'd Sculls to pay the *joiners* themselves.

But what is it to me, *who paid for it*? or *by what means* it came to make such a figure, as it now does, both within doors and without? It becomes me better, as an historian, to acquaint posterity what uses it is put to, and what *momentous* affairs are transacted within its walls.

Daniel Defoe, c.1723

Daniel Defoe (c.1660–1731) is of course famous as the author of Robinson Crusoe, but he was also a leading intellectual and political agitator, and a pioneer of journalism writing hundreds of works of all kinds. As a young man he had been part of the Monmouth rebellion to overthrow James II. His most successful work after Crusoe was *A Tour thro' the Whole Island of Great Britain*, published between 1724 and 1727. Although he sometimes drew upon his own past, or antiquarian works such as Camden's *Britannia*, he certainly based his numerous accounts of 'circuits' on real journeys. His visit to Oxford (recounted in Letter 6) was on the way to Anglesey. The text here is from a 1927 edition.

From hence I came to Oxford, a name known throughout the learned world; a city famous in our English history for several things, besides its being an university.

1. so eminent for the goodness of its air, and healthy situation; that our Courts have no less than three times, if my information is right, retir'd hither, when London has been visited with the pestilence; and here they have been always safe.
2. It has also several times been the retreat of our princes, when the rest of the kingdom has been embroil'd in war and rebellion; and here they have found both safety and support; at least, as long as the loyal inhabitants were able to protect them.
3. It was famous for the noble defence of religion, which our first reformers and martyrs made here, in their learned and bold disputations against the Papists, in behalf of the Protestant religion; and their triumphant closing the debates, by laying down their lives for the truths which they asserted.
4. It was likewise famous for resisting the attacks of arbitrary power, in the affair of Magdalen College, in King James's time; and the Fellows laying down their fortunes, tho' not their lives, in defence of liberty and property.

This, to use a scripture elegance, is that city of Oxford; the greatest (if not the most antient) university in this island of Great-Britain; and perhaps the most flourishing at this time, in men of polite learning, and in the most accomplish'd masters, in all sciences, and in all the parts of acquir'd knowledge in the world.

I know there is a long contest, and yet undetermin'd between the two English universities, about the antiquity of their foundation; and as they have not decided it themselves, who am I? and what is this work? that I should pretend to enter upon that important question, in so small a tract?

It is out of question, that in the largeness of the place, the beauty of situation, the number of inhabitants, and of schollars, Oxford has the advantage. But fame tells us, that as great and applauded men, as much recommended, and as much recommending themselves to the world, and as many of them have been produced from Cambridge, as from Oxford.

Oxford has several things as a university, which Cambridge has not… For example, the theater, the museum, or chamber of rarities, the Bodleian Library, the number of colleges, and the magnificence of their buildings are on the side of Oxford…

It is a noble flourishing city, so possess'd of all that can contribute to make the residence of the scholars easy and comfortable, that no spot of ground in England goes beyond it. The situation is in a delightful plain, on the bank of a fine navigable river, in a plentiful country, and at an easy distance from the capital city, the port of the country. The city itself is large, strong, populous, and rich; and as it is adorn'd by the most beautiful buildings of the colleges, and halls, it makes the most noble figure of any city of its bigness in Europe.

To enter into the detail or description of all the colleges, halls, &. would be to write a history of Oxford, which in so little a compass as this work can afford, must be so imperfect, so superficial, and so far from giving a stranger a true idea of the place; that it seems ridiculous, even to think it can be to any ones satisfaction…

[Defoe nonetheless then lists all of the colleges and details of their foundation.]

…I shall now give a summary of what a traveller may be suppos'd to observe in Oxford, *en passant*, and leave the curious inquirer to examine the histories of the place, where they may meet with a compleat account of every part in the most particular manner, and to their full satisfaction.

There are in Oxford 17 colleges, and seven halls, some of these colleges as particularly, Christ Church, Magdalen, New College, Corpus Christi, Trinity, and St John's will be found to be equal, if not superior to some universities abroad; whether we consider the number of the scholars, the greatness of their revenues, or the magnificence of their buildings.…

Besides the colleges, some of which are extremely fine and

magnificent; there are some publick buildings which make a most glorious appearance: The first and greatest of all is the theatre, a building not to be equall'd by any thing of its kind in the world; no, not in Italy itself: Not that the building of the theatre here is as large as Vespasian's or that of Trajan at Rome; neither would any thing of that kind be an ornament at this time, because not at all suited to the occasion, the uses of them being quite different.

We see by the remains that those amphitheatres, as they were for the the exercise of their publick shews, and to entertain a vast concourse of people, to see the fighting of the gladiators, the throwing criminals to the wild beasts, and the like, were rather great magnificent bear-gardens, than theatres, for the actors of such representations, as entertain'd the polite part of the world; consequently, those were vast piles of building proper for the uses for which they were built....

The theatre at Oxford prepared for the publick exercises of the schools, and for the operations of the learned part of the English world only, is in its grandeur and magnificence, infinitely superiour to any thing in the world of its kind; it is a finish'd piece, as to its building, the front is exquisitely fine, the columns and pilasters regular, and very beautiful; 'tis all built of freestone: The model was approv'd by the best masters of architecture at that time, in the presence of K. Charles II. who was himself a very curious observer, and a good judge; Sir Christopher Wren was the director of the work, as he was the person that drew the model: Archbishop Sheldon, they tell us, paid for it, and gave it to the university: There is a world of decoration in the front of it, and more beautiful additions, by way of ornament, besides the antient inscription, than is to be seen any where in Europe; at least, where I have been.

The Bodleian Library is an ornament in it self worthy of Oxford, where its station is fix'd, and where it had its birth. The history of it at large is found in Mr. speed, and several authors of good credit; containing in brief, that of the old library, the first publick one in Oxford, erected in Durham now Trinity College, by Richard Bishop of Durham, and Lord Treasurer to Ed. III. it was afterward joined to another, founded by Cobham Bishop of Worcester, and both enlarg'd by the bounty of Humphry Duke of Gloucester, founder of the divinity schools: I say, these libraries being lost, and the books embezzled by the many changes and hurries of the suppressions in the reign of Hen. VIII. the commissioner appointed by King Edw. VI. to visit the universities, and establish the Reformation; found very few valuable books or manuscripts left in them. In this state of things, one sir Thomas Bodley, a wealthy and learned knight, zealous for the encouragement both of learning and religion, resolv'd to apply, both his time, and estate, to the erecting and furnishing a new library for the publick use of the university.

In this good and charitable undertaking, he went on so successfully, for so many years, and with such a profusion of expence, and obtain'd such assistances from all the encouragers of learning in his time, that having collected books and manuscripts from all parts of the learned world; he got leave of the university, (and well they might grant it) to place them in the old library room, built as is said, by the good Duke Humphry. To this great work, great additions have been since made in books, as well as contributions in money, and more are adding every day; and thus the work was brought to a head, the 8th of Nov. 1602, and has continued encreasing by the benefactions of great and learned men to this day: To remove the books once more and place them in beauty and splendor suitable to so glorious a collection, the late Dr. Radcliff has left a legacy of 40000 *l.* say some, others say not quite so much, to the building a new repository or library for the use of the university: This work is not yet built, but I am told 'tis likely to be such a building as will be greater ornament to the place than any yet standing in it…

Other curious things in Oxford are, the museum, the chamber of rarities, the collection of coins, medals, pictures and antient inscriptions, the physick-garden, &c.

The buildings for all these are most beautiful and magnificent, suitable for the majesty of the university, as well as to the glory of the benefactors.

William Mildmay, 1738

Sir William Mildmay (1705–71) of Moulsham was a landowner in Essex, created a baron as well as sheriff of Essex in 1765, and had earlier been involved with settling the boundaries of Nova Scotia. He kept a journal of his travels in Wales, now held at Essex Record Office (shelfmark D/DMy/15M50/1325).

Dr. Ratcliff has left forty thousand pounds, to Build a new Library for the better disposition of the Books, its now Building, and its said to be done after a finer Plan than the Vatican at Room, or that at Paris; but I own by what I cou'd see of it I thought it seem'd to be a Heavy, Clumsey Building; tho' to be sure it will be a fine one when its finished.

The Printing House is removed from the Top of the Theatre where it formerly was, to a New one that was Built on the Profits of my Lord Clarrendons History, & call'd the Clarrendon Printing House, it is Built with stone, and has an exceeding good Front North, & south, with Pillers of the Dorick Order.

The Museum is also a Handsome Building the Front to the

street is 60 Foot, it contains a Collection of Natural Curiositys, Roman Antiquities, & Medals, with Curious Agats, & other stones: the particulers of wich tis impossible to remember: Here is the skull of Oliver Cromwell; and a Mummy of great Antiquity.

Thomas Salmon, 1744

Thomas Salmon (1679–1767) was a prolific writer on history and topography. His 1744 work *The Present state of the Universities, and of the five adjacent Counties of Cambridge, Huntingdon, Bedford, Buckingham, and Oxford* in fact only covered Oxford, but gave much information beyond the usual details of the university.

OXFORD is situated on a small Eminence, almost encompass'd with Meadows, except on the East; these Meadows are about a Mile over, beyond which are Hills of a moderate Heighth bounding the Prospect from the Town.

Towards the East, there is a continued Ascent of two Miles' to the Top of a high Hill, which goes by the Name of *Shotover-Heath;* from whence there is a fine Prospect of the City and adjacent Country, as there is also from the Hills on the West.

The whole Town, including the suburbs, is a Mile in length from East to West, and almost as much in breadth from North to south, being three Miles in Circumference, but it is of an irregular Figure, and many void spaces are comprehended within these Limits, besides the numerous Courts and Gardens belonging to the respective Colleges.

The City, properly so called, formerly surrounded by a Wall, is of an oblong Form, and not much more than two Miles in Circumference; *Magdalen College* with the Eastern as well as the Northern suburbs, which contain the Parishes of *Holywell, Magdalen, St Clements* and St *Giles's*, with *Baliol, Trinity, St John's* and *Wadham* Colleges, are without the old Walls, of which there are but very small Remains at present, but the Fortifications and Outworks rais'd by the Royalists in the Time of the late Civil Wars, included all the suburbs. Those Fortifications however could not cover the City from the Enemies shot, and it is not easy to conceive how *Oxford* should have sustain'd a long siege, unless the Garrison within was almost as numerous as the Army which invested it.

The Town lies so much expos'd to the shot of an Enemy, from the Hills on the East, that it might have been beat down in twenty-four Hours if the Assailants had attempted it, and there is no reason to be given why they did not when *Fairfax* lay before it, but the Respect the Enemy's Generals had for these seats of Learning…

But to return to the present Town, the Gates on the East and North are still left standing, though the Walls are almost entirely demolish'd, as well as the Fortifications erected by the Royalists in the Time of the Civil Wars; the Castle also, which stands at the West End of the Town, no longer deserves that Name, the Ruins whereof now serve for the County Goal, as the North Gate (which has obtain'd the Name *of Bocardo)* does for the Town Goal, but why this Gate or Prison is called *Bocardo,* I could never learn.

The Principal street of the City runs from East to West, almost the length of the Town, but under different Names; the East End goes by the Name of *High-street*, the middle of it is call'd the *Old Butcher-Row*, and the West End *Castle-street:* The East End forms a very spacious street, clean and well pav'd, and illuminated with Lamps in the Winter; it is adorn'd with the

Fronts of three fine Colleges, *viz. University, Queens* and *All-Souls*, the University Church of St *Mary's*, and the new beautiful Church of *All-Saints*; but the private Houses are meanly built and very much diminish the Beauty of it. I do not remember six Houses in this fine street, built either with brick or stone; the Houses which stand East of that elegant Edifice of *Queen's* College, would disgrace an ordinary Market-Town. It is observable that this celebrated street is very crooked, which some indeed admire as a Beauty, having a mighty Gust for serpentine streets, as well as serpentine Rivers. Another thing which takes off much from its beauty is the *Butcher-Market*, held here every *Wednesday* and *Saturday*, when the stalls extend half the length of this fine street, and indeed there are no other Market-Places in *Oxford* than the great streets: As the Butchers take up this, the Farmers incumber the other principal streets with their Waggons and Corn, and Fish and Poultry are sold in both. Another great Nusance is the Dirt which People bring out of their Houses, and lay in the middle of the street in heaps every Morning.

The second street in *Oxford*, is that which runs from south to North, crossing the street already describ'd about the Middle, from whence that part of the Town has obtain'd the Name of *Quater Vois* or the four Ways, corruptly call'd *Carfax*; as the Corporation Church, which stands near the four Ways likewise is, though it is something difficult to conceive, how the Word *Carfax* was form'd out of those two *French* Words, *Quater Vois.*

The south End of this second street is called *Fish-street*, and the other End of it the *Corn-Market;* from whence we pass through *Bocardo,* or the North-Gate, into *Maudlin* Parish and St *Giles's*, which form a very spacious street, and in some Respects preferable to either of the former: On the East side of *Fish-street,* stands that noble College of *Christ-Church,* the magnificent Front whereof is extended an hundred and twenty Yards. some of the private Buildings here, and in that part of this street called the *Corn-Market,* are preferable to those of the *High-street.*

But the pleasantest part of the Town, especially for those that love Retirement, is St *Giles's*, which lies without the North-

Gate; this has all the Advantages of Town and Country, it is broader than the *High-street,* well planted with Elms on each side and better built, several of the Houses being of white hewn stone; and in this street also stand the Colleges of *Baliol* and St *John's.* A stranger would be apt to expect indeed, that this City was generally built with stone, their Quarries lying but two Miles distant from it, *viz. at Hedington* or *shotover Heath;* but still it seems it is cheaper building with Brick than stone at *Oxford;* there are two or three private Houses now building of Brick in the *High-street,* by *London* Undertakers, and I am inform'd they bring all their Bricks up the *Thames* from *London,* which is above an hundred Miles by Water. As to the generality of the Inhabitants, they don't think it worth their while to build either with Brick or stone on College Leases, and this is the true Reason the private Buildings are for the most part so mean in this, as well as in the other University of *Cambridge.* The Lessees patch up their Clay Tenements as long as they can, and sometimes chuse to let their Leases run out, rather than be at the Charges of renewing them and repairing their Houses.

I should have taken Notice, that the City of *Oxford* is almost encompass'd with Rivers, or rather with several Branches of the Rivers *Isis* and *Cherwell,* insomuch that *Oxford* is not to be approach'd except on the North, but by Bridges, which lie over these streams; and this has made some People imagine that the City is very strongly situated, not reflecting that it is commanded by the rising Grounds on the East, and that it is of too great an Extent to be regularly fortified in every Part.

It is needless, after this Account of the situation of *Oxford,* to observe that it is well supply'd with Water, which they do not trouble themselves to fetch from the Rivers that surround it, but every House almost has a Pipe laid in, which supplies them with *Thames* Water as it is usually call'd here; for the common People both here and in the Country above *Oxford,* give the River *Isis* the Name of *Thames,* and scarce know it by any other Name, as has been intimated already; though the *Thames* does not fall into the Isis till it has pass'd *Oxford* many Miles, and I find one street of the City goes by the Name of *Thames-street,* namely that which runs down to the *High-Bridge.*

The chief Bridges are, First, *East-Bridge,* which lies over the River *Cherwell,* being the grand Avenue from *London:* The second lies over the *Isis,* on the south side of the Town, being the Avenue from *Abington* and *Berkshire*; and the Third is the *High-Bridge* over the same River *Isis,* in the West-part of the Town; besides which, there are some lesser Bridges, with Causeys running from them near a Mile in length, cross the Meadows which encompass the Town; for their Meadows lying under Water part of the Winter, *Oxford* cannot be approach'd on the West but by such Causeys, which leads me to enquire into the Healthfulness of the situation, so mightily cryed up by Dr. *Plot,* (who has written the natural History of Ox*fordshire)* as well as by the present' Inhabitants and scholars who reside here.

From what I have observ'd, (and I have spent some time at *Oxford* in almost every season of the Year,) the City is generally Healthful; but towards the latter End of the Year, and in wet Winters, the poor People who can neither afford good Liquor or Firing, are pretty much subject to Agues; nor is it to be much wonder'd at, since *Oxford,* like *Venice*, in a wet season, appears surrounded with Water, if we take a View of it from *Shotover-Hill;* even Doctor *Plot,* who has written a Panegyrick on *Oxford,* acknowledges the Water frequently hangs too long in the Meadows, and this must be admitted by every one that has seen it in a wet season; but then an ingenious Gentleman observ'd to me, that these Waters which cover their Meadows, have a quick Current, and that running Waters are not unwholsome; adding, that wherever there is a Current of Water, there is a Current of Air, and that it is only the stagnation of Waters which render them Unhealthful: To which it is answered, that though it be admitted there is a Current in the Meadows, when the Floods are at the Heighth, yet when the Water grows low there must be a stagnation, from whence Vapours will arise that are not very salutary: It is observable also, that these Meadows lie chiefly on the south and West-part of the City, from which Points the

Winds usually blow, and consequently the Air of the Town must be very moist when the Meadows are cover'd with Water, which may not however have such ill Effects on that part of the Inhabitants who eat and drink well, as on the poorer sort, who cannot afford good Liquor or Firing enough to keep them warm, in a Place where Fuel is so excessive dear; Coals being usually sold for Fifteen-pence the Bushel, and sometimes a great deal more, and Wood is still dearer.

Freidrich von Kielmansegge, 1761

Freidrich von Kielmansegge (1728–1800) was a German count from Hanover, whose lively travel writings were published in 1902 as *Diary of a Journey to England in the Years 1761-1762*, translated by his great-grandson's wife. His son, also Freidrich, fought at the Battle of Waterloo.

Having nothing more to see here, we drove that same afternoon on to Oxford. We employed the whole of the 26th, as well as the 27th up to noon, seeing the sights of Oxford, which I will now briefly describe in succession. The town itself, situated on high ground, is an English mile long, and just as broad, including the large pleasure-grounds, which are near the colleges and suburbs. A fine and very wide street passes through the whole length of the town, which contains few good houses, with the exception of the colleges and public buildings. The size of the town may be judged from the fact that it includes fourteen parishes. St Mary's Church is the so-called University church, where the members attend to hear the sermon on Sundays and holy days. When viewed from outside, it is rather a fine building to look at. All

Souls' Church is handsomer, and is ornamented outside with Corinthian pillars. It is said to be very fine inside, and has no pillars to support the vaulted roof, which is of considerable height. It is asserted that there existed a university in Oxford as early as 872.

The famous Bodleian Library is the principal sight to see. It is supposed to be the largest in Europe, excepting the one in the Vatican at Rome. *[He then describes the collections.]*

The so-called public school forms a square, with one wing as a library. In the middle of the principal facade, where the Savile Library is placed, is a large archway with a turret over it, which contains an observatory.

Close to this building is the theatre, which is almost in the shape of a D. It is ornamented outside with sculpture, consisting of the statues of Charles II., the old Duke of Ormond, and Archbishop Sheldon. Inside are portraits of the two last-named and of the builder of this edifice, the famous Christopher Wren. All the other paintings on the ceiling have been taken down for repairs, and the whole building was filled with scaffoldings, so I cannot say more about it than that the public lectures are held here, and that it is considered one of the best buildings in Oxford, having been erected, at a cost of 15,000, in 1669, by Archbishop Sheldon, who bequeathed a further £2000 towards its maintenance. The ceiling is flat, and made of short beams, fitted into each other in such a way that they are supported only by the walls on the side, and by one another, although the width is seventy feet and the length eighty feet.

Close by is the Ashmolean Museum, which is a building in modern style, of freestone (a quarry stone), sixty feet long, very much ornamented, and with a splendid Corinthian portico; it was built for the University by Christopher Wren, in 1683. It contains a collection of natural history specimens, which was presented in the same year to the University by Sir Ellis Ashmole, from whom the museum derives its name. subsequently, several others have given it rich collections of Egyptian hieroglyphics and other curious antiquities, animals and herbs collected in China, curious manuscripts, an entire mummy, and a good library; so it is quite worth while seeing. It is only a pity that so little time is allowed to strangers in such places, that they can only see everything superficially, and cannot give sufficient attention to the objects of most interest. In addition to this, it must be remarked that generally, and especially England, the people who show you over such places are porters, or caretakers, who seldom know much about them, merely show visitors round, and are glad when they leave. They earn their money so easily that they show you nothing at all, or only such objects as they consider worth seeing, which are usually well-known things, and to be seen every day in any collection; so that the rarest objects often escape the eye, and remain unobserved…

On the other side of the theatre is the Clarendon printing-house, which was erected in the year 1711, from the profits realized by the sale of Lord Clarendon's History, the manuscript of which his sons, the Lords Clarendon and Rochester, had given to the University. It is built of stone, is 115 feet long, and has a fine Doric portico, the columns of which reach to the height of both stories. On the roof stand figures of the nine Muses, and above the entrance a statue of Lord Clarendon. The whole building is occupied by the printing-offices of the University. In one room hangs a fine portrait of Queen Anne, by Kneller. In return for the fee you give to see the whole building, you receive a well-executed woodcut, with your name printed on it, surrounded with ornaments.

The most costly and the handsomest building is the Radcliffe Library. This new edifice stands by itself, in the middle of a large square, surrounded by small obelisks and lamps, and cost £42,000, 2000 more than the founder, Dr. John Radcliffe, a physician, had intended. He also gave £100 a year for the purchase of new books, and another 100 for keeping up the whole institution. The building is in the form of a rotunda, or, to be more correct, consists of sixteen angles. Eight of these angles are prettily decorated, and seven of them have real entrances with doors, whilst the doorway in the eighth, behind which is the stair-case, is false. The whole measures 100 feet in diameter. The upper story is ornamented outside with double Corinthian columns, and windows and niches alternating. A handsome gallery with a balustrade runs all round, and the whole is surmounted by a fine cupola.

Beautiful and splendid as it all is, and however much you may admire this gallery on entering, your admiration decreases when you see how few books there are, compared with the quantity which so extensive a building leads you to expect. The number is so small that the man who shows you over voluntarily makes an excuse for this, stating that all the volumes have not yet been put in their places; but as the building was finished in 1749, there would have been time enough to place them there. But for this drawback, I do not believe that a similar institution could be found anywhere, for at one glance you look over an enormous library placed in a handsome building.

The large botanical garden for herbs and plants is situated in the suburbs, opposite Magdalen College, and was presented to the University by the Earl of Denbigh, in 1632. His statue, and those of Charles I. and Charles II., stand in niches over the large and fine gateway, which Inigo Jones designed. In the garden, all kinds of native and foreign plants and herbs which can be cultivated in the open air are to be found, and some very rare ones in hot and cold glass-houses. At the time of our visit one very tall aloe, seventy-seven years old, was just flowering in the open ground, where it had been planted several years before, without having suffered, as the result showed. Two enormous pedestals, with flower-pots and flowers, each cut out of one single stem of yew, stood on either side of a broad walk, which, with a high avenue of the same trees, do not produce a bad effect.

As to the colleges, there are altogether twenty in Oxford, namely, Magdalen, Queen's, New, University, All Souls', Brasenose, Lincoln, Jesus, Exeter, Trinity, Balliol, St John's, Wadham, Corpus, Merton, Oriel, Christ Church, Pembroke, Worcester, and Hertford; there are also five halls, St Alban's, St Edmund's, New Inn, St Mary's, and Magdalen. These differ from the colleges in that each does not form so compact a body in itself, and has also no special funds, but is only supported by the fees of the students, who merely swear that they will observe the rules of the halls.

All the members wear a black gown, made in the shape of an open domino; in addition to this they have a peculiar head-gear, which consists of a black and tight-fitting cap, covered by a flat square lid or top, one point of which is worn in front. There are small differences in the costume, such as black silk in some of the gowns, and silver or gold tassels fastened on the hats, which mark distinctions of class, as well as the grades amongst the various members of the University.

The principal work in all of the colleges being very similar, we contented ourselves by seeing six or eight of the best... *[He gives extensive details of these visits – a few highlights of college customs recounted are below.]*

Queen's College... It is the custom in this college, on Sundays and holidays, for one of the students to stand up during dinner-time and make a speech on a theological subject, and one on philosophical sciences on weekdays.

A curious custom exists here; on New Year's Day every member receives a needle and thread from the housekeeper, with these words, "Take this and be chary of it" in allusion to the name of the founder of the college, Robert Egglefield (*aiguille fit*). The call to table is given by a trumpet.

New College... A hedge with a low arch adds considerably to the charm of a large garden, which is laid out daintily. A number of students walk round the court at noon and again at six in the evening, calling everybody in French to their meals, in these words, "*A manger tous seigneurs.*"

Christ Church... At the entrance, in the middle, is a large tower designed by Christopher Wren, and containing a big bell, called Tom, which is sounded every night at nine o'clock when the students have to be at home, each in his own college. I was told that 101 strokes were given each time, being the number of rooms for students in this college...

I have mentioned the most interesting things which were shown us in these colleges. Although there are always many interesting objects to be found if you have time to go and see them all, we were unable to remain longer, as we had little time at our disposal.

James Woodforde, 1771-75

James Woodforde (1740–1803) was a clergyman whose extensive and detailed diaries of country life were published in the 1920s as The Diary of a Country Parson. Woodforde (who was related to Robert Woodforde – see the entry for 1639) studied in Oxford from 1758 for five years, and then returned from 1773 to 1776. His Oxford diaries were published as *Woodforde at Oxford 1759–1776* in 1969.

[This short item from 19th October 1771 records major restructuring in Oxford – for further details see http://www.oxfordhistory.org.uk/broad/history/mileways_act.html]

The Streets in Oxford are much improved, all the Signs are taken down and put against the Houses, the Streets widened, East-Gate & Bocardo taken down & a new Bridge going to be built where Magdalen Bridge now stands, and temporary Bridges during the building of it now making by Christchurch Broad-Walk, for to go up the Hill &c.

. . .

[And here, on March 13th 1775, Woodforde records seeing a hanging.]

I breakfasted, dined, supped & slept again & at Coll: Cooke fasted with me this morning. At half past eleven this morning went with Cooke to see George Strap hanged—who was hung about a Qr before one o'clock near the Castle. He confessed (just as he came out of the Castle) the Crime for which he suffered, but not before. He pulled up his Cap two or three Times to delay. A Methodist prayed by him in the Cart for some Time under the Gallows—He seemed full hardy. It is the declared Yesterday, if he had only his Liberty for one Qr of an Hour, he would employ it in murdering of his Wife. I think I never saw such Sullenness & Villainy in one Face. Jack Ketch *[i.e. the hangman]* kissed him twice before he went of[f]. His Body was carried to Dr Parsons's to be dissected, and anatomized pursuant to the Sentence. I do believe that there were more than six Thousand Spectators present when he was hanged.

Thomas Quincey, 1772

Thomas Quincey (d.1793) was a Manchester textile merchant, and was the father of the well-known essayist Thomas de Quincey. He wrote 'A tour in the Midland Counties of England, performed in the summer of 1772', printed in several episodes in the *Gentleman's Magazine* in 1774.

Oxford is so well described in several books… that it would be mere plagiarism to mention anything concerning it, except a few curious observations added to those accounts.

In the first, it is said, that "the private buildings are neat, and the public ones sumptuous." That the public edifices are truly noble is past contradiction; but the private houses are far more deserving the character of neatness, except in the High-street, and a very few others; indeed, so far from it, that in most of the streets, the houses are of timber plastered over, some of them built in a barbarous old method, the upper stories projecting forward; yet, in regard to this last article, not so ugly as in other towns I have seen.

In the suburb at the entrance from London, is an hospital for diseased persons, where none can be admitted (as I was told) but such whose cure is judged capable of being effected or furthered by a medicinal spring within the building. It is a neat, well-built edifice.

The remains of the castle at Oxford are a strong, square tower, and a large artificial mount, the latter now ornamented with trees on the top: there is nothing singular in the construction of the tower, but from the mount is a most enchanting prospect: on one hand the city appears beneath you, and with its numerous spires, domes, &c. raises an idea of vast magnificence; on the other side is a fine extended vale, rich in verdure and wood, terminated by lofty hills, and nobly decorated by the Isis, serpentizing along to some distance, then losing itself behind a variety of objects, and afterwards appearing again in one open sheet of water; the whole exhibits a charming scene of native beauty, heightened by some additional strokes of art.

The streets of this city are well lighted, and excellently paved with the smaller sort of those pebbles which are generally used for that purpose; the foot-walks leading from the town to some distance, are handsomely gravelled.

Ascending the first hill in the London road, you have a fine view back into the vale, of the city, surrounded by wood and gardens, of the neighbouring country, and of the river just presenting itself in several spots.

Georg Christoph Lichtenberg, 1775

Georg Christoph Lichtenberg (1742–99) was a German physicist who also wrote satires. He visited England in 1770 and 1774–5, and his accounts from letters and diaries were translated in 1938 as *Lichtenberg's Visits to England.*

Mr. Hornsby, the Professor of Astronomy at Oxford, entertained me in his house for two days and presented me with a valuable work, namely, the tables published by the Board of Longitude to facilitate the calculation of the distances observed between the [moon] and fixed stars. The book is a small folio and five inches thick. This Observatory surpasses that at Richmond as much as the latter does the Göttingen one. I have persuaded Mr. Hornsby to learn German, and he will do so. Can you imagine, my dear Sir, a telescope through which stars of the fifth, and even of the sixth, magnitude can be seen, sometimes in broad daylight, for example, at four o'clock on a summer afternoon. This can be done with Mr. Hornsby's transit instrument. I had heard of it before, but thought there must be some misunderstanding, until this honest man, who is certainly is no boaster, told me of it, and had seen through the telescope Alkor, the middle star in the Great Bear's tail, so clearly at one o'clock in the afternoon that it could scarcely escape notice. When I was in Oxford the weather was not favourable enough for this, although it served for other observations. If this kind of thing goes on, the astronomers will at length be able to go to bed at night like other craftsmen. 12,000 thalers are to be spent on the Observatory at Oxford.

Thomas Campbell, 1775

Thomas Campbell (1733–95) was an Irish clergyman whose journal of his visit to Britain was rediscovered in Australia in 1854, and published in 1947 as Dr Campbell's Diary of a Visit to England in 1775. It includes some frank descriptions of his encounters with samuel Johnson.

We went to the Coffee house in the evening where almost all the Gownsmen we saw were tipsy, & the streets reechoed with bacchanalian crys as we returned from supper… The next night also we went to another Coffee house & there the scene was only shifted – all muzzy. This happily abated my enthusiasm conceived for an Oxford education; for such was the venerability of the place that after taking a cursory view of it I was almost in a paroxism of superstition…

A gownsman of Oxford thus painted the fellows of All Souls —They lived so luxuriously & indolently that they did nothing but clean their teeth all the morning & pick them all the evening.

Karl Moritz, 1782

Karl Phillipp Moritz (1756–93) was a German writer and editor who began his career as a hatter's apprentice, then an actor, before he turned to writing and travel. He wrote of his visit to England in a series of letters. The text here is from an 1886 edition of *Travels in England in 1782*.

Beguiling the tediousness of the road by such discourse, we were now got, almost without knowing it, quite to Oxford.

[My travelling companion] told me I should now see one of the finest and most beautiful cities, not only in England, but in all Europe. All he lamented, was, that on account of the darkness of the night, I should not immediately see it.

This really was the case: "And now," said he, as we entered the town, "I introduce you into Oxford by one of the finest, the longest, and most beautiful streets, not only in this city, but in England, and I may safely add in all Europe."

The beauty and the magnificence of the street I could not distinguish; but of its length I was perfectly sensible by my fatigue; for we still went on, and still through the longest, the finest, and most beautiful street in Europe, which seemed to have no end; nor had I any assurance that I should be able to find a bed for myself in all this famous street. At length my companion stopped to take leave of me, and said he should now go to his college.

"And I," said I, "will seat myself for the night on this stone bench and await the morning, as it will be in vain for me, I imagine, to look for shelter in a house at this time of night."

"Seat yourself on a stone!" said my companion, and shook his head. "No, no! come along with me to a neighbouring ale-house, where it is possible they mayn't be gone to bed, and we may yet find company." We went on a few houses further, and then knocked at a door. It was then nearly twelve. They readily let us in; but how great was my astonishment, when, on being shown into a room on the left, I saw a great number of clergymen, all with their gowns and bands on, sitting round a large table, each with his pot of beer before him. My travelling companion introduced me to them, as a German clergyman, whom he could not sufficiently praise for my correct pronunciation of the Latin, my orthodoxy, and my good walking.

I now saw myself in a moment, as it were, all at once transported into the midst of a company, all apparently very respectable men, but all strangers to me. And it appeared to me extraordinary that I should, thus at midnight, be in Oxford, in a large company of Oxonian clergy, without well knowing how I had got there. Meanwhile, however, I took all the pains in my power to recommend myself to my company, and in the course of conversation, I gave them as good an account as I could of our German universities, neither denying nor concealing that, now and then, we had riots and disturbances. "Oh, we are very unruly here, too," said one of the clergymen as he took a hearty draught out of his pot of beer, and knocked on the table with his hand. The conversation now became louder, more general, and a little confused; they enquired after Mr. Bruns, at present professor at Helmstadt, and who was known by many of them.

Among these gentlemen there was one of the name of Clerk, who seemed ambitious to pass for a great wit, which he attempted by starting sundry objections to the Bible. I should have liked him better if he had confined himself to punning and playing on his own name, by telling us again and again, that he should still be at least a Clerk, even though he should never become a clergyman. Upon the whole, however, he was, in his way, a man of some humour, and an agreeable companion.

Among other objections to the scriptures, he started this one to my travelling companion, whose name I now learnt was Maud, that it was said in the Bible that God was a wine-bibber. On this Mr. Maud fell into a violent passion, and maintained that it was utterly impossible that any such passage should be found in the Bible. Another divine, a Mr. Caern referred us to his absent brother, who had already been forty years in the church, and must certainly know something of such a passage if it were in the Bible, but he would venture to lay any wager his brother knew nothing of it.

"Waiter! fetch a Bible!" called out Mr. Clerk, and a great family Bible was immediately brought in, and opened on the table among all the beer jugs.

Mr. Clerk turned over a few leaves, and in the book of Judges, 9th chapter, verse xiii, he read, "should I leave my wine, which cheereth God and man?"

Mr. Maud and Mr. Caern, who had before been most violent, now sat as if struck dumb. A silence of some minutes prevailed, when all at once, the spirit of revelation seemed to come on me, and I said, "Why, gentlemen, you must be sensible that it is but an allegorical expression;" and I added, "how often in the Bible are kings called gods!"

"Why, yes, to be sure," said Mr. Maud and Mr. Caern, "it is an allegorical expression; nothing can be more clear; it is a metaphor, and therefore it is absurd to understand it in a literal sense." And now they, in their turn, triumphed over poor Clerk, and drank large draughts to my health in strong ale; which, as my company seemed to like so much, I was sorry I could not like. It either intoxicated or stupefied me; and I do think it overpowers one much sooner than so much wine would. The conversation now turned on many other different subjects. At last, when morning drew near, Mr. Maud suddenly exclaimed, "D-n me, I must read prayers this morning at All-Souls!" D-n me is an abbreviation of G-d d-n me; which, in England, does not seem to mean more mischief or harm than any of our or their common expletives in conversation, such as O gemini! or, The deuce take me!

Before Mr. Maud went away, he invited me to go and see him in the morning, and very politely offered himself to show me the curiosities of Oxford. The rest of the company now also dispersed; and as I had once (though in so singular a manner) been introduced into so reputable a society, the people of the house made no difficulty of giving me lodging, but with great civility showed me a very decent bed-chamber.

I am almost ashamed to own, that next morning, when I awoke, I had got so dreadful a headache, from the copious and numerous toasts of my jolly and reverend friends, that I could not possibly get up; still less could I wait on Mr. Maud at his college.

The inn where I was goes by the name of the Mitre. Compared to Windsor, I here found prince-like attendance. Being, perhaps, a little elevated the preceding evening, I had in the gaiety, or perhaps in the vanity of my heart, told the waiter, that he must not think, because I came on foot, that therefore I should give him less than others gave. I assured him of the contrary. It was probably not a little owing to this assurance that I had so much attention shown to me.

I now determined to stay at least a couple of days at Oxford; it was necessary and proper, if for no other reason, yet merely that I might have clean linen. No people are so cleanly as the English, nor so particular about neat and clean linen. For, one afternoon, my shirt not having been lately changed, as I was walking through a little street, I heard two women, who were standing at a door, call after me, "Look at the gentleman there! a fine gentleman, indeed, who cannot afford even a clean shirt!"

I dined below with the family, and a few other persons, and

the conversation in general was agreeable enough. I was obliged to tell them many wonderful stories (for who are so illiterate or insensible as not to be delighted with the marvellous!) concerning Germany and the King of Prussia. They could not sufficiently admire my courage in determining to travel on foot, although they could not help approving of the motive. At length, however, it came out, and they candidly owned, that I should not have been received into their house, had I not been introduced as I was.

I was now confirmed in my suspicions, that, in England, any person undertaking so long a journey on foot, is sure to be looked upon and considered as either a beggar or a vagabond, or some necessitous wretch, which is a character not much more popular than that of a rogue…

Monday I spent at Oxford, but rather unpleasantly, on account of my headache. Mr. Maud himself came to fetch me, as he had promised he would, but I found myself unable to go with him.

Notwithstanding this, in the afternoon, I took a little walk up a hill, which lies to the north of Oxford; and from the top of which I could see the whole city; which did not, however, appear to me nearly so beautiful and magnificent as Mr. Maud had described it to me during our last night's walk.

The colleges are mostly in the Gothic taste, and much overloaded with ornaments, and built with grey stone; which, perhaps, while it is new, looks pretty well, but it has now the most dingy, dirty, and disgusting appearance that you can possibly imagine.

Only one of these colleges is in the modern style. The houses of the city are in general ordinary, in some parts quite miserable; in some streets they are only one story high, and have shingled roofs. To me Oxford seemed to have but a dull and gloomy look; and I cannot but wonder how it ever came to be considered as so fine a city, and next to London.

I remained on the hill, on which there was a flight of steps that led to a subterraneous walk, till sunset, and saw several students walking here, who wore their black gowns over their coloured clothes, and flat square hats, just like those I had seen worn by the Eton scholars. This is the general dress of all those who belong to the universities, with the exception of a very trifling difference, by which persons of high birth and rank are distinguished.

It is probably on account of these gowns that the members of the university are called Gownsmen, to distinguish them from the citizens, who are called Townsmen… This dress, I must own, pleases me far beyond the boots, cockades, and other frippery, of many of our students. Nor am I less delighted with the better behaviour and conduct which, in general, does so much credit to the students of Oxford.

The next morning Mr. Maud, according to his promise, showed me some of the things most worthy of notice in Oxford. And first he took me to his own room in his own college, which was on the ground floor, very low and dark, and resembled a cell, at least as much as a place of study. The name of this college is Corpus Christi. He next conducted me to All Souls' College, a very elegant building, in which the chapel is particularly beautiful. Mr. Maud also showed me, over the altar here, a fine painting of Mengs, at the sight of which he showed far more sensibility than I thought him possessed of. He said that notwithstanding he saw that painting almost daily, he never saw it without being much affected…

Afterwards Mr. Maud conducted me to the Bodleian Library, which is not unworthy of being compared to the Vatican at Rome; and next to the building which is called the Theatre, and where the public orations are delivered. This is a circular building with a gallery all round it, which is furnished with benches one above the other, on which the doctors, masters of arts, and students sit, and directly opposite to each other are erected two chairs, or pulpits, from which the disputants harangue and contend.

Christ Church and Queen's College are the most modern, and, I think, indisputably the best built of all the colleges. Balliol

College seems particularly to be distinguished on account of its antiquity, and its complete Gothic style of building.

Mr. Maud told me that a good deal of money might be sometimes earned by preaching at Oxford; for all the members of a certain standing are obliged in their turn to preach in the church of the university; but many of them, when it comes to their turn, prefer the procuring a substitute; and so not unfrequently pay as high as five or six guineas for a sermon.

... Going along the street we met the English poet laureate, Warton, now rather an elderly man; and yet he is still the fellow of a college. His greatest pleasure next to poetry is, as Mr. Maud told me, shooting wild ducks.

... At the Mitre, the inn where I lodged, there was hardly a minute in which some students or others did not call, either to drink, or to amuse themselves in conversation with the daughter of the landlord, who is not only handsome, but sensible, and well behaved.

They often spoke to me much in praise of a German, of the name of Mitchel, at least they pronounced it so, who had for many years rendered himself famous as a musician. I was rejoiced to hear one of my countrymen thus praised by the English; and wished to have paid him a visit, but I had not the good fortune to find him at home.

Hannah More, 1782

Hannah More (1745–1833) was a religious writer, philanthropist and anti-slavery campaigner. She was a friend of Samuel Johnson – in this scene from 1782, published in *Memoirs of the Life and Correspondence of Mrs. Hannah More* (1834), Dr Johnson shows her his old rooms in Oxford.

Oxford, June 13, 1782. You cannot imagine with what delight he showed me every part of his own College (Pembroke), nor how rejoiced Henderson looked, to make one in the party. Dr. Adams, the master of Pembroke, had contrived a very pretty piece of gallantry. We spent the day and evening at his house. After dinner Johnson begged to conduct me to see the College, he would let no one show it me but himself, — 'This was my room; this Shenstone's.' Then after pointing out all the rooms of the poets who had been of his college, 'In short,' said he, 'we were a nest of singing-birds. — Here we walked, there we played at cricket.' He ran over with pleasure the history of the juvenile days he passed there. When we came into the common room, we spied a fine large print of Johnson, framed and hung up that very morning, with this motto: 'And is not Johnson ours, himself a host.' Under which stared you in the face, 'From Miss More's Sensibility.' This little incident amused us; but alas ! Johnson looks very ill indeed — spiritless and wan. However, he made an effort to be cheerful, and I exerted myself much to make him so.

Stebbing Shaw, 1788

The Rev. Stebbing Shaw (1762–1802) was an antiquarian, diarist and topographer, particularly for Staffordshire. He published *A Tour to the West of England in 1788* in 1789. His brief note on Oxford opts to avoid the standard subjects and unusually mentions the prison.

Besides the wonderful improvements that have been made, within a few years, by widening the streets, paving, &c. the new county gaol does great credit to the Spirit of the place, and when finished will be one of the strongest and best in the kingdom. Its situation is adjacent to the old castle, and encompassed by massy stone wall, which we enter at a large tower and gateway, over which is to be the platform for executions. In the centre of this spacious area, stands the governor's house, whence he can overlook the whole of the buildings under his care. The principal one for felons is divided into 60 cells, eight feet by seven, strong as iron and stone can make them. The two lefter Bridewells contain 20 each, and are almost finished. The old castle is to remain as it was, so that the whole group which is of that style of architecture, will have a noble appearance. There is also a city prison now building upon the same plan.

Edward Daniel Clark, 1791

Edward Daniel Clarke (1769–1822) was a clergyman, mineralogist and travel writer. He travelled across Europe, Asia and Africa, as well as closer to home – this critical account of Oxford is from his *Tour through the south of England and part of Ireland made during the summer of 1791*, published in 1793.

Oxford, from Woodstock, is not marked by any particular beauty. The country, bleak, champaign and fat, consists of those features which *melancholize* the environs of its sister seminary. It is not in the power of nature to assume a visage more deformed than she wears in the neighbourhood of Oxford and Cambridge. Not one expressive line, not one interesting object, presents itself to the traveller's eye and the desponding Freshman, as he sojourns across the drear expanse, feels the full force of Johnson's assertion, when, speaking of scotland, he says "that, if the miserable aspect of the country should induce a man to hang himself, he would scarcely find a tree to swing from!"

I shall confine my remarks upon this city within a very small compass—it is foreign to my present purpose to record, in pompous detail, its colleges and the history of their founders: few are unacquainted with our Universities: and those, who wish to acquire a more accurate knowledge of their buildings and benefactors, will find ampler sources of information in the *Oxford and Cambridge Guides* than in any laboured essay of mine.

In Oxford there seems, what may be styled, *a disease of buildings*. The traveller is presented with a profusion of edifices jumbled together with no great display either of taste or design. It is a kind of anarchy in stone and mortar, where every thing is confused; and architecture, in a high fever, seems to have stuck one edifice here and another there, varying the nonconformity of her work in proportion to her delirium. There is a *Mausoleum* for a *library*, and a *cock-pit* for *public disputants*. There is a *sepulchre* of *manuscripts*, and a long gallery, where heroes with ugly faces, and learned graduates in full bottomed wigs, are copiously displayed upon canvas.

What shall be said of CHRIST-CHURCH? where neat little PECKWATER cements the dirty puddle and the leaden mercury that disgraces its neighbouring quadrangle—and of the boasted THEATRE? with its wrong side foremost, that turns its back upon the public and hides its fine front in a corner and of St MARY's? with a low gothic spire, but of sufficient beauty for every one to wish it taller—and of the prospect from the top of RADCLIFF's empty LIBRARY? where the view of ALL-SOULs alone is recompence for the fatigue of ascending.

Robert Southey, 1793

Robert Southey (1774–1843) was a Romantic poet, a friend of Samuel Taylor Coleridge, and Poet Laureate from 1813. This description of a visit to Oxford is from a letter he wrote to G.C. Bedford on 16th March 1793 (published in *Letters of Robert Southey*, 1912).

On the water I went yesterday, in a little skiff, which the least deviation from the balance would overset. To manage two oars and yet unable to handle one! My first setting off was curious. I did not step exactly in the middle, the boat tilted up, and a large barge from which I embarked alone saved me from a good ducking; my arm, however, got completely wet. I tugged at the oar very much like a bear in a boat; or, if you can conceive anything more awkward, liken me to it, and you will have a better simile. When I walk over these streets what various recollections throng upon me, what scenes fancy delineates from the hour when Alfred first marked it as the seat of learning!

Bacon's study is demolished, so I shall never have the honour of being killed by its fall; before my window Latimer and Ridley were burnt, and there is not even a stone to mark the place where a monument should be erected to religious liberty. I have walked over the ruins of Godstow Nunnery with sensations such as the site of Troy or Carthage would inspire; a spot so famed by our minstrels, so celebrated by tradition, and so memorable in the annals of legendary, yet romantic, truth. Poor Rosamond! some unskilful impostor has painted an epitaph upon the chapel wall, evidently within this century; the precise spot where she lies is forgotten, and the traces are still visible of a subterranean passage perhaps the scene of many a deed of darkness…

George Woodward, 1796

George 'Moutard' Woodward (1765–1809) was a caricaturist and humorist, whose many works included *Eccentric Excursions in England and South Wales*, with drawings etched by Isaac Cruikshank.

Nothing can be more entertaining , than the various groupes of strangers repairing to view the colleges, who are daily seen parading the streets of this city of learning , preceded by one of those meagre figures usually appointed as guides and orators on the occasion. For a representation, see Plate 47 *[below]*…

There are several good inns, the principal are the Cross, the Star, and the Angel. By taking down the Conduit in High-street, a great improvement is made in that part of the city. — The Magistrates are the CHANCELLOR, High Steward, Vice Chancellor, two Proctors, a Public Orator, a Keeper of the Archives, a Register, three Squire Beadles, three Yeoman Beadles, and a VERGER.

I shall in this place take advantage of my original plan, and confine particulars to the two extremities. The CHANCELLOR is usually one of the principal nobility, and chosen by the university; the nobleman who at present holds that honourable office is the Duke of Portland. — The office of the VERGER is on solemn occasions to walk before the Vice-Chancellor and Beadles with a silver rod in his hand, (see Plate 48, *below*). This sketch is not meant to represent any particular characters, but merely to give the reader some conception of University Processions…

There is scarcely an engraving… but what represents a student with the cap in his hand pointing to some particular building, or parading the streets with his brethren of the gown. As this mode of representation is grown so very common, I shall take the liberty of deviating so far from the beaten track, as to introduce two imaginary characters, which I hope for the honour of the university, will never be realized, viz. A Conceited Fellow and a Drunken Fellow of different colleges. (see Plate 49.)

… How simple a thing is nature unadorned, and how much ought the generality of mankind to be indebted to the first inventor of wigs.—Of this I had a curious instance during my stay at Oxford. In passing a barber's shop, I perceived a lusty figure with a plain bald head, under the hands of an operator somewhat similar in appearance to Razor, in the farce of the Upholsterer; nothing was visible of the patient, but the upper part of his face, the lower being obscured by a copious lather; and the body was closely environed, by a Cloth *large enough for a table at a corporation dinner!*—In this situation the figure presented nothing particularly remarkable in respect to consequence, but in a few hours after I accidentally met with the same person contemplating a curious plant, in the physic gardens. I immediately recollected him, by his prominent eye-brows, and was afterwards told by the gardener, that the AUGUST PERSONAGE in question, was nothing less than a Proctor!—The tremendous explanation operated like an electric shock, and I could not help again repeating to myself how much ought the generality of mankind to be indebted to the inventor of wigs!

In order to illustrate the subject more fully, the Plates 52 and 53 represent a *Proctor without a Wig*, and a *Proctor with a Wig*!

Absorbed in contemplation on these useful coverings of the

head, I proceeded through several streets, till at length I arrived at a miserable little shop , where amongst other articles was a second-hand WIG for sale , though by its appearance it seemed to have weathered several generations, yet some marks of its ancient beauty were still discernible…

George Thompson, 1798

George Thompson describes himself in one book as a "schoolmaster of the Esk Bank Academy" (presumably in Scotland) but other details are elusive. As well as a travel journal of a visit to the Isle of Man, he wrote *A Sentimental Tour, Collected from a Variety of Occurrences, from Newbiggin, near Penrith, Cumberland, to London, by Way of Cambridge; and from London to Newbiggin, by Way of Oxford, &c.*, which adopts a merry and light-hearted tone.

ARRIV'D at Oxford, a few lines introduce me to the good offices of a certain gentleman, in whose composition generous sympathy appear'd to make a principal ingredient. I had scarcely seen the Oxonian, till I felt myself—at home. He takes me by the hand. He eyes my interest. He espouses my case,—He introduces me, and my interests to his fellow students,—and other colleges;—his fellow students are pleas'd, at his instance, to smile propitious on my undertaking. The senior Gentlemen also of Queen's meet my object and are polite, as are such other colleges, as I had time to address.

They were good, indeed! They who of all the world, had the

least need of books—they purchase my London publication and they (from politeness and humanity) subscribe to my Sentimental Tour; and I have to trust they will not forget to exert their good offices in behalf of such Brother-authors, as chance, with an honourable plea, or notable erudition, with fair pretensions, may, in future, throw on their patronage.

Animated in my literary attempt by great and learned characters Here, it remains for me to exert my best, but poor abilities —poor! among learned men…

See! Magdalene's fine Addisonian half serpentine range of alcove regaling peripatetic ground, begirt with elm, and many a less notic'd, yet not ignoble wood, which crowds the scene.

Here the Students walk, and converse hold. See! one young Student, grown wan—nay, old with books, and bookish cares, in wakeful dream solitary musing. Now behold a group of Livelies, all sleek and trim, in full career chattering along, and patting the shoulder of the son of *reverie*—"Cheer up, old Boy, join in company, and mend thy pace; let social glee unbend thy mind…"

… I join the Queen's men to a gradually rising ground, call'd Headington, eastward from Oxford; which is the most pleasant, the most regaling, and genius- –and health- – inspiring walk in the place…

Arriv'd at the extremity of their usual ambulation, they shew me an aged elm with huge half-decayed arms. It was upon this tree (may we hope they said in jest) a certain member of our University sported at his own expence—with a rope…

I'm now in the Grove where the majestic elms please the eye —nay, more—screen from heat. The deer walk in this grove with a philosophic air—graze, and recumbent rest, not solicitous for *to-morrow*, happy in their neighbours—but far happier in their liberal portion of temperate fare! O, would man but copy here!

George Lipscomb, 1799

George Lipscomb (1773–1846) was an English doctor and antiquarian, who is known for a history of Buckinghamshire and a number of works of travel and topography. This lyrical stroll through Oxford was published in his *Journey into South Wales*, 1802.

Having changed horses at Tetsworth, we soon reached Oxford; and, like poor Moritz (the Prussian divine, who made a pedestrian excursion from London into Derbyshire) flopped at the Mitre, but did not find the "prince-like attendance there," which that gentleman was so fortunate as to meet with.

The indisposition of one of the passengers, added to the inconvenience occasioned by the closeness of our stowage, induced me to quit the stage at this place; and it being now about three o'clock in the morning, there was some difficulty in procuring a bed, particularly as the inn seemed to be left to the entire management of the waiters and coachmen.

Disgusted by their incivility, and perhaps a little nettled by the preference which was given to a young gentleman, who alighted from the roof of the coach, and whom, from his careless air, and the manner in which he swore, I presumed to be a collegian, I determined to seek lodgings at another inn; whither I caused my portmanteau to be conveyed immediately, and where I was lucky enough to find a comfortable apartment.

After a short repose, I prepared to take a walk round this venerable city; whose beauties are so numerous and attractive, that every traveller is prompted to attempt their description, although the talk requires a master's hand.

It was vacation time, and a kind of void seems to strike one with pensive musing. An air of calm tranquillity is given to the buildings, the walks, and even the inhabitants. I enter *Christ Church*, where the ear so often listens with delight and admiration, to the full-flowing periods, and the refined learning of men, justly famed for literary acquirements; and where friendship is crowned with the joyous festivity of a convivial board.

All is now serene composure, and melancholy stillness creeps along the walls. The mirth-resounding cloister is now forsaken; and even the fountain in the quadrangle has ceased to play.

I stroll through the venerable grove, and along the high o'erarching vista: I court the gentle stream of Isis, and wind my solitary way along the margin of her devious course.

Thus wandering through the glade, the dear images of long lost friends arise before me; and as the fleeting visions pass, "the grateful memory of the good" awakens the mind to those glorious pat[t]erns of departed excellence, which have been afforded us in their example.

Charles Dibdin, 1801-2

Charles Dibdin (1745–1814) was a prolific composer, novelist and actor. *Observations on a tour through almost the whole of England, and a considerable part of Scotland in a series of letters* was published c.1803. He gives the usual description of Oxford's buildings and colleges, and ends on this sombre note…

I shall therefore say nothing further on the subject of this university than to express the sorrow I feel that it cannot, for I suppose it cannot, operate so as to embrace all the purposes suggested by that wisdom, and carried into execution by that magnificence, which dictated such admirable institutions.

Surely it ought to be possible, during the short space taken for the terms, that the exactest order should be kept, and all that time, so precious to the interest and welfare of the student, should be soberly and industriously employed. Instead of this, unfortunately the inns in term time are constantly filled with riots, and one would think that fathers sent their sons to the university to plunge them into extravagance, and disqualify them for the study of everything but profligacy and brutality. I speak through the knowledge of what I saw fourteen years ago, when the etiquette of rioting was estimated; when the price of a waiter's broken head was two guineas, breaking knees of a horse three; when a troop of Italian singers were invited into the town against the express order of the vice-chancellor, and when the mayor, who soberly remonstrated with them upon their outrageous conduct, was struck by one of the students. These are the circumstances which will always operate as a drawback upon our universities and in favour of those in SCOTLAND, for a Scotch man is too much an economist of his time to idle it away improvidently.

Mary Anne Eade, 1802

Mary Anne Eade came from a London merchant, and is only known through her *Journal of a tour from Clapton through North Wales to Ireland*, a trip she undertook with her husband William. The original, written for her sister, is held by the National Library of Wales and has been digitised at https://editions.curioustravellers.ac.uk/doc/0013

Friday 18th [June] – We had a pleasant ride this morning (which was remarkably fine) to Oxford before breakfast, & took this first meal very comfortably at the star which seemed to be an excellent Inn; & when we had finished it we took a man from the Inn to shew us the most remarkable colledges &c: The first we visited was Christ Church where there is a large gallery of fine pictures by the ancient masters; many of these I should liked to bestow a much longer time on, than our [leisure] would allow & I reluctantly left them to follow our conductor to the hall, which is large & handsome & hung round (as is often the case) with portraits of eminent men who have sprung from the colledge. We then ascended to the library which is also large, consisting of two stories & built of Norway oak which has a solid & venerable appearance: this colledge is an ancient & fine one, but I saw little in it to please, altho I traversed it with interest from considering it was here our dear William would probably acquire all the "academic lore" he will one day I hope possess. From hence we passed to the Radcliffe Library an elegant circular building with which I was greatly pleased: we exhibited ourselves "selon l'usage" on the leads, & had from them a very fine view of this beautiful city, which gratified [me] extremely –

With the Bodleian Library I was much disappointed having somehow acquired an idea of its being a very beautiful as well as large repository of the works of the learned; I suppose I was mistaken in imagining it to be esteemed such, at least it appeared to me quite the reverse, & the old ceiling painted all over with the arms of the University I thought positively ugly; its size was also inferior to my expectations & I was surprized how its 200,000 volumes could all find places; particularly as so much space is occupied by the pictures, of which I admired some very much, but was most struck by a noble statue in brass of William Earl of Pembroke the graceful ease of which cannot be surpassed. We next, I believe, visited Magdelen Chapel with which I was delighted: the entrance is lighted only by painted glass windows, the greater part of which have been lately executed by Egerton, in one color a dark brown; they are extremely beautiful & cast a chastened gloom over the chapel which adds an inexpressible awe to the inexplicable feelings of mingled gratitude, devotion & piety which it is impossible not to experience while gazing on the exquisite picture by Guidaover the communion table; of our saviour bearing his cross; the patient anguish, the dignified resignation, the "something not of this earth," that seemed breathed over the whole figure, made it appear "no work of mortal hand;" a more touching performance imagination cannot conceive.

The New Colledge Chapel was the last object of our curiosity; it is I think in all respects well worthy of admiration but the celebrated window painted by Jervais from a design of sir Joshua

Reynolds, is certainly its most beautiful ornament. the upper part represents the Nativity & the lower (divided into seven compartments) the christian & cardinal virtues; I prefered the figures designed for the christian graces, but could not decide in my own mind, whether the group so sweetly figuring Charity, or the enchanting personification of Hope delighted me most. After seeing this window I no longer hesitated to allow the superiority of Jervais to Girton, but perhaps he owes it more to the noble design from which he copied than to his own excellence.

We just passed thro' the Christ Church & Magdelen Walks, which are pretty enough, but not equal to Clare Hall Piece at Cambridge nor did any single thing at Oxford delight me as much as The Kings Colledge Chapel & Trinity Library there, yet as a whole I infinitely prefer this to its sister University, its colledges [*sic*] are altogether much handsomer, & more advantageously situated; indeed I can imagine nothing finer in its kind than the High street where so many of them stand. I felt some regret at not entering University Colledge, tho' assumed it contained nothing worthy of notice, but age & my veneration for its founder, the noble Alfred, would have made it an object of curiosity to me, & I could not look at it without interest. After seeing all this variety of objects I returned to our Inn, with my head in compleat confusion, which I could not get rid of while eating an excellent nooning of which some pretty good ice formed a part…

C.A.G. Goede, 1802-3

Christian Augustus Gottlieb Goede was the author of *The Stranger in England, or, Travels in Great Britain*, published in 1807. He offers a brief and dismissive account of England's most famous universities…

Oxford and Cambridge, the two celebrated universities of this country, consist of ranges of ill-contrived colleges. The student differs little from the school-boy, excepting, that, instead of being punished with a rod, he is punished by a longer task than usual. The former certainly has more liberty, but still he lives in the college under the care of a tutor; he must be present at appointed hours of instruction in the public hall, and regularly attend divine service; he reads the ancients, but the sciences are not within the limits of college instruction. There are professors, certainly, who give public lectures on these subjects, but none of distinguished fame or literary reputation.

Benjamin Silliman, 1805-6

Benjamin Silliman (1779–1864) was an American chemist and one of the first professors of science in the country. He studied in Edinburgh in 1805, and kept a journal of his travels, published in 1812 as *A journal of travels in England, Holland and Scotland.*

The fatigue of travelling through the night prevented my rising in season for the morning service; but, in the afternoon, I went to the church of St Mary, an ancient Gothic structure, belonging to Queen's College. The officers and students of this college attended, and we had the best sermon which I have heard in England. I suppose the gentleman who delivered it was the Professor of Theology. His discourse was, in sentiment, correct, and in style manly, perspicuous, and elegant.

The officers and students all wear a loose black gown over their dress, which is like that of other gentlemen. They wear a black a velvet cap, fitting the head exactly, like the crown of the hat before the modern high hats came into fashion. This cap is destitute a of a rim or border, of any kind, either for ornament or use, and thus the face and eyes are completely ex. posed to the weather. On the very pinnacle of the cap. is fixed a square board, covered also with black; it looks as a thin book would do, if laid on the crown of the head. From the middle of this, a tassel falls over on one side of the head. This is usually black, but, in the case of noblemen, it is of gold, and there are other variations in the singular costume which have described, intended to designate academic as well as civil rank. The effect of the whole is some what ludicrous, at the same time that it is grave and even solemn. When the members of the university are out of Oxford, they throw off this garb, and appear like other men.

At the inn where I lodged, I accidentally met Mr. D— We had been at Yale College together, some years ago, and neither of us, I believe, would have thought of our meeting at Oxford. We of course became associates; for it was an interesting discovery to find an old acquaintance where one supposed himself surrounded only by strangers, and we agreed to travel to London together. Towards evening we made, in part, the circuit of Oxford and its environs, and viewed the exterior of most of the academic buildings, and the interior of some. The buildings are generally the form of hollow square; the included space forms a court which is commonly verdant and beautiful. In one of the chapels we saw a curious production of art. It was a picture of a man, made by tracing the lines on a board with hot poker. We were informed that one of the fellows, by amusing himself with burning a board with this instrument, gradually passed to attempting rude delineations, and ultimately acquired s0 much skill, as to leave this monument of his singular taste behind him; it is by no means deficient in elegance and effect.

Oxford is a place of great grandeur and beauty. It is situated in the midst of a country whose verdure is very rich and luxuriant. It stands at the intersection of the Thames and Cherwell, and these rivers and the canals are bordered by gravel walks, and rows of ancient, lofty, and venerable trees these are so numerous in the town, that the buildings are often overshadowed by them, and appear as if in a forest. The whole town has an unrivalled air of magnificence and dignity. No place ever impressed me with such feelings of admiration and awe, and I presume it is with. out a parallel in the world. Instead of the narrow and dirty lanes of trading towns, and the confused noise of commerce, there are spacious and quiet streets, with fine houses, of stone, built in a very good taste. But what produces the principal effect is the great number of academic buildings, in a style of much grandeur, and rendered venerable by strong marks of antiquity. The effect is very much heightened by the frequent avenues of lofty forest-trees, and by the historical associations naturally connected a with a university which claims Alfred the Great for its founder. The most considerable of the colleges here is that Christ Church, founded by Cardinal Wolsey; and the most extensive and beautiful walk is in the rear of this.

Oxford contains nearly 12,000 inhabitants. It was distinguished for its strong partiality to Charles I. who held his court here daring the whole of the civil wars. It is built principally on two streets, which cross each other at right angles, and the high street is considered as one of the finest in Europe. It is terminated by a beautiful bridge. The circumference of Oxford is said to be three miles, and its form circular. My travelling book says that there are thirteen parish churches, but I did not see them all. The number of colleges and other similar institutions is twenty-five. They informed me that the number of students in the university was about 1200, and that Christ Church college has more than any other. There is a fashion in these things, and the nobility and men of fortune are found principally at Christ Church.

Sophia Hoare, 1808

Sophia Hoare (1771–1824, née Thrale) was the daughter of the Welsh diarist and patron of the arts Hester Thrale (later Piozzi) and her husband Henry Thrale, a wealthy brewer and politician (altogether they had 12 children). Sophia was a favourite of his father's close friend Samuel Johnson. she married the banker Henry Merrick Hoare in 1807. The text here is the Oxford part from her Journal of a Tour into N. Wales – the original is held by the Hoare & Co. bank archives and has been digitised at editions.curioustravellers.ac.uk/doc/0018

We left London July 29. 1808 and arrived at Oxford by six O'Clock to Dinner: The Roads were delightful from the Rain that had fallen, after the very hot Weather we had experienced, and it was more like a refreshing agreeable Airing, than a Journey which in general I have no particular fancy for. I wrote a Note to our Friend Mr P. who had promised to be our Guide in seeing the Lions, to give notice of our Arrival, and asked him to Breakfast with us the following Morning, that we might have plenty of time before us, to see all that was curious & entertaining. We went first to the Theatre, a large Circular Building, where the Prize Poems are recited in the presence of the Chancellor who is seated in the Centre of the semi circular part, the Nobleman & Doctors on his right & left hand, with the Proctors & Curates in their Robes, Master of Arts, Batchelors & Under Graduates in their respective habits & places, together with strangers of both sexes: making in all when filled upwards of 4000 Persons.

The Building is adorned with statues of the Founder Archbishop Sheldon and the Duke of Ormond likewise Sir Christopher Wren the Architect; The Roof of the Theatre is very remarkable, being supported without Pillars although it is 80 Feet one way by 90 the other and only sustained by the side Walls. Our next Visit was to the Logic & Moral Philosophy Schools where there is a very fine Collection of statues, Marbles, Busts &c. We saw likewise the Clarendon Printing office built in 1711 with the profits arising from L.d. Clarendon's *History* – It is a most noble Edifice 115 feet in length & consists of two lofty stories – On the Top are statues of the Nine Muses, and over the Entrance a statue of the Earl of Clarendon.

The Radcliffe Library was our next Object and very well worth seeing it is – It stands in a fine Area and Dr. John Radcliffe left the sum of 40,000 Pounds to build it and provide a Librarian with a salary… There are an immense Number of Books, which are continually increasing as one Hundred a Year is appropriated to the buying of Books – There are two superb Roman Candlesticks in this Library, given to the University by sir Roger Newdigate found in the Ruins of the Emperor Adrian's Palace at Tivoli, in the Campagna Romana.

We went next to Christ Church College where our Guide left us for a short time while he went about some business of his own, which gave us an Opportunity of examining the fine Collection of Pictures… The Stair Case and Entrance to this College have lately been greatly Altered & improved by Mr Wyatt, and the Hall is by far the most magnificent Room of the kind in Oxford: the Roof framed of Timber curiously wrought. The Kitchen is likewise well worth seeing – In the Church of this College which is the Cathedral of the Diocese is some fine Painted Glass, and in the Tower, which makes a singular and beautiful Appearance on the outside of the Building are ten Celebrated Bells including the Great One called Tom, which weighs eight Tons & a half on the sound of which the scholars of the University use to retire to their respective Colleges…

The beautiful Gardens and Walks belonging to the Colleges pleased me as much as any part of it only that I grew very much tired at last with seeing and hearing so much. – New College however I was highly delighted with – the Chapel especially and the Great Window with Sir Joshua's beautiful designs painted by Jarvis.

… We went into the Garden Court which is separated from the garden by an Iron Gate & Pallisade where we unluckily shut ourselves in and if we had not happen to find a student sitting reading in the Alcove who kindly lent us his Key, we might have been detained longer than we wished. The Bodleian Library was unfortunately shut, so we only saw the Picture Gallery where there was nothing very remarkable except a beautiful Mary Queen of Scots by Vandyke…

I was extremely pleased with Magdalen College & Chapel the Windows of which are very fine – There is a very large Altar Piece of the last Judgement and underneath it a very fine Picture of our saviour bearing his Cross supposed to be by Guido & reckoned the finest Picture in the World, brought into England by the late Duke of Ormond… the Grove and Gardens belonging to this College are delightful and it contains about 40 head of Deer.

We walked some time in the Water Walks as they are called by the side of the little River that surrounds the Paddock – After having seen all this thoroughly we returned to our Inn the star where we remained to rest ourselves a few minutes and then Mr Pigou came again to conduct us to Dinner at his Chamber at Merton College which he likewise showed us. We met at Dinner a Friend of his an agreeable Man, and after taking another Walk in Merton College Gardens which are beautiful and quite private we stepped into our Chaise where I fell fast asleep and never woke till I arrived at Chapel House, where we drank Tea and slept.

William Cobbett, c.1821

William Cobbett (1763–1835) was a journalist, MP and farmer who campaigned for lower taxes, the reversal of land enclosure and the abolition of rotten boroughs in Parliament. His *Rural Rides* was first published in serial form in the 1820s, and then as a book in 1830 – it describes his journeys across the south and Midlands of England on horseback to understand rural conditions.

Sunday Nov 18th:… Upon beholding the masses of buildings, at Oxford, devoted to what they call "*learning*" I could not help reflecting on the drones that they contain and the wasps they send forth. However, malignant as some are, the great and prevalent characteristic is *folly*: emptiness of head; want of talent; and one half of the fellows who are what they call *educated* here, are unfit to be clerks in a grocer's or mercer's shop. As I looked up at what they call *University Hall*, I could not help reflecting that what I had written, even since I left Kensington on the 29th of October, would produce more effect, and do more good in the world, than all that had, for a hundred years, been written by all the members of this University, who devour, perhaps, not less than a *million pounds a year*, arising from property, completely at the disposal of the "Great Council of the Nation"; and I could not help exclaiming to myself: "stand forth, ye big-wigged, ye gloriously feeding Doctors! stand forth, ye *rich* of that church whose *poor* have had given them a *hundred thousand pounds a year*, not out of your riches, but out of the *taxes*, raised, in part, from the *salt* of the labouring man! stand forth and face me, who have, from the pen of my leisure hours, sent, amongst your flocks, a hundred thousand sermons in ten months! More than you have all done for the last half century!" I exclaimed in vain. I dare say (for it was at peep of day) that not a man of them had yet endeavoured to unclose his eyes.

Harriette Story Paige, 1839

Harriette Story Paige (1809–63) came from Massachusetts, USA. she and her husband accompanied the American lawyer and statesman Daniel Webster on a trip to Europe in 1839. Her journal of the British leg was published in 1917 as *Daniel Webster in England.*

MONDAY, July 15. Angel Inn, Oxford. We reached this place at six o'clock p.m., after a most agreeable drive from London of 54 miles, through the most charming and cultivated country. In consequence of a great agricultural celebration to-morrow, the Inn, where we are, is crowded to excess, but we have a spacious parlour and comfortable sleeping-rooms… We came here "en prince" as they choose to call it, that is, we used for the first time, the travelling carriage in which we propose going, next week to Scotland. Four post horses, with two postillions, in blue jackets, and yellow topped boots; the horses changed every ten miles; our maid, and man servant, Hamilton and Holton in the "rumble" behind. Mr. Webster, from preference, occupied the coach box, and the ladies, the carriage proper, which, in spite of the "imperial" (containing our dresses, on the top), was partially open, it being a landau, which admits of this arrangement…

July 16. Oxford. Immediately after breakfast, we sallied forth to see the colleges, which are twenty-three in number. We first visited Magdalen (they pronounce it *Maudlin*) College, and Christ's Church College, founded by Cardinal Wolsey. The Magdalen Chapel is very beautiful; the Gothic stone cuttings, even to the organ case are very fine, and the oak carvings extremely well done… This college is on a small stream called "Isis." On our way to Christ's Church College, we walked through a long avenue of trees called "Addison's walk," commanding a view of a park, and some fine deer. Addison was a fellow of Magdalen College, and in one of the rooms, our guide informed us, "there were six chairs, on which he had often sat."

Most of the colleges are built of brick, in the form of quadrangles, and one is constantly surprised at their extent, and the wealth required to support such extensive establishments. They are all independent of each other. You enter an arched way, either in a lofty hall, or through the lower part of a building, and at once, you are in a spacious quadrangle, sometimes a verdant, grassy square, with chapel, commons, and library around. These seem the very place for quiet study, and repose. Their look of solemnity is very attractive. Most of the chapels are really very beautiful…

The quadrangle of "Queen's College" directly opposite our lodgings, has been temporarily covered, and converted into an immense dining-room, and tables are laid, to accommodate eighteen hundred persons. Earl Spencer is to preside, he being a great agriculturist.

July 17, Oxford. Drove with Kenyon, to "Blenheim" this morning, the seat of the Duke of Marlborough…

As we alighted from our carriage, at the Angel Inn, on our return, we encountered Mr. Hamilton, waiting eagerly for our appearance, to take us, by a private passage, to the Provost's house, the windows of which, open upon the college quadrangle, and command a view of the tables, and arrangements for the dinner of to-day. There were several ladies, evidently dressed for the occasion, and while we were there, the procession entered, and Mr. Webster's plate, was the third one, on the right, from the President of the day, the princely owner of "Althorp." … I am now writing by the open window, and am constantly interrupted by the shouts of the multitude, the clapping of hands, and the fine music of the band, in the adjoining quadrangle.

Nathaniel Hawthorne, 1856

Nathaniel Hawthorne (1804–64) was an American novelist, famous for *The Scarlet Letter* and other stories. From 1853 to 1857 he was the United States consul in Liverpool. These accounts of Oxford are from *Passages from the English Note-books*, 1872.

June 11th. … Oxford is an ugly old town, of crooked and irregular streets, gabled houses, mostly plastered of a buff or yellow hue; some new fronts; and as for the buildings of the University, they seem to be scattered at random, without any reference to one another. I passed through an old gateway of Christ Church, and looked at its enclosed square, and that is, in truth, pretty much all I then saw of the University of Oxford. From Christ Church we rambled along a street that led us to a bridge across the Isis; and we saw many row-boats lying in the river,—the lightest craft imaginable, unless it were an Indian canoe. The Isis is but a narrow stream, and with a sluggish current. I believe the students of Oxford are famous for their skill in rowing.

To me as well as to J—— the hot streets were terribly oppressive; so we went into the Roebuck Hotel, where we found a cool and pleasant coffee-room. The entrance to this hotel is through an arch, opening from High Street, and giving admission into a paved court, the buildings all around being part of the establishment,—old edifices with pointed gables and old-fashioned projecting windows, but all in fine repair, and wearing a most quiet, retired, and comfortable aspect. The court was set all round with flowers, growing in pots or large pedestalled vases; on one side was the coffee-room, and all the other public apartments, and the other side seemed to be taken up by the sleeping-chambers and parlors of the guests. This arrangement of an inn, I presume, is very ancient, and it resembles what I have seen in the hospitals, free schools, and other charitable establishments in the old English towns; and, indeed, all large houses were arranged on somewhat the same principle.

By and by two or three young men came in, in wide-awake hats, and loose, blouse-like, summerish garments; and from their talk I found them to be students of the University, although their topics of conversation were almost entirely horses and boats. One of them sat down to cold beef and a tankard of ale; the other two drank a tankard of ale together, and went away without paying for it,—rather to the waiter's discontent. Students are very much alike, all the world over, and, I suppose, in all time; but I doubt whether many of my fellows at college would have gone off without paying for their beer…

August 31st. … Mr. S. C. Hall met us at the Oxford station, and under his guidance we drove to a quiet, comfortable house in St Giles Street, where rooms had been taken for us. Durham, the sculptor, is likewise of the party.

After establishing ourselves at these lodgings, we walked forth to take a preliminary glimpse of the city, and Mr. Hall, being familiar with the localities, served admirably as a guide. If I remember aright, I spoke very slightingly of the exterior aspect of Oxford, as I saw it with J—— during an hour or two's stay here, on my way to Southampton (to meet S—— on her return from Lisbon). I am bound to say that my impressions are now very different; and that I find Oxford exceedingly picturesque and rich in beauty and grandeur and in antique stateliness…

In the High Street, which, I suppose, is the noblest old street in England, Mr. Hall pointed out, the Crown Inn, where Shakespeare used to spend the night, and was most hospitably welcomed by the pretty hostess (the mother of Sir William Davenant) on his passage between Stratford and London. It is a three-story house, with other houses contiguous,—an old timber mansion, though now plastered and painted of a yellowish line. The ground-floor is occupied as a shoe-shop; but the rest of the house is still kept as a tavern. . . .

We rambled pretty extensively about the streets, sometimes seeing the shapes of old edifices dimly and doubtfully, it being an overcast night; or catching a partial view of a gray wall, or a pillar, or a Gothic archway, by lamplight. . . . The clock had some time ago struck eleven, when we were passing under a long extent of antique wall and towers, which were those of Baliol College. Mr. D——— led us into the middle of the street, and showed us a cross, which was paved into it, on a level with the rest of the road. This was the spot where Latimer and Ridley and another Bishop were martyred in Bloody Mary's time…

After lunch to-day we (that is, Mrs. Hall, her adopted daughter, S——-, and I, with the Ex-Mayor) set forth, in an open barouche, to see the remarkables of Oxford, while the rest of the guests went on foot. We first drew up at New College (a strange name for such an old place, but it was new some time since the Conquest), and went through its quiet and sunny quadrangles, and into its sunny and shadowy gardens. I am in despair about the architecture and old edifices of these Oxford colleges, it is so impossible to express them in words… people have very free admittance; and many parties of young men and girls and children came into the gardens while we were there.

These gardens of New College are indescribably beautiful, —not gardens in an American sense, but lawns of the richest green and softest velvet grass, shadowed over by ancient trees, that have lived a quiet life here for centuries, and have been nursed and tended with such care, and so sheltered from rude winds, that certainly they must have been the happiest of all trees. Such a sweet, quiet, sacred, stately seclusion— so age-long as this has been, and, I hope, will continue to be—cannot exist anywhere else. One side of the garden wall is formed by the ancient wall of the city, which Cromwell's artillery battered, and which still retains its pristine height and strength. At intervals, there are round towers that formed the bastions; that is to say, on the exterior they are round towers, but within, in the garden of the College, they are semicircular recesses, with iron garden-seats arranged round them. The loop-holes through which the archers and musketeers used to shoot still pierce through deep recesses in the wall, which is here about six feet thick…

Leaving New College, Bennoch and I, under Mr. Parker's guidance, walked round Christ Church meadows, part of our way lying along the banks of the Cherwell, which unites with the Isis to form the Thames, I believe. The Cherwell is a narrow and remarkably sluggish stream; but is deep in spots, and capriciously so,—so that a person may easily step from knee-deep to fifteen feet in depth. A gentleman present used a queer expression in reference to the drowning of two college men; he said "it was an awkward affair." I think this is equal to Longfellow's story of the Frenchman who avowed himself very much "displeased" at the news of his father's death. At the confluence of the Cherwell and Isis we saw a good many boats, belonging to the students of the various colleges; some of them being very large and handsome barges, capable of accommodating a numerous party, with room on board for dancing and merry-making. Some of them are calculated to be drawn by horses, in the manner of canal-boats; others are propellable by oars…

John Henry Parker, 1873

John Henry Parker (1806–84) was an archaeologist and writer on architecture, known for his work on the history of Rome. In 1860 he published *The Railway Traveller's Walk through Oxford*, accompanied by numerous engravings, and a later edition in 1873. The full book, offering a detailed tour of the sights of Oxford, can be found online at Google Books, but here is his introductory 'Notice to the stranger, &c.' and the map from the back cover.

On arriving at Oxford by the Railway, it would be advisable for the stranger to proceed at once in an omnibus or other conveyance to CHRIST CHURCH, as a starting-point,—the present *western* entrance to the city from the station being unfortunately through the worst part of the town.

The original and *eastern* entrance to Oxford, in the old coach-days, was over Magdalen Bridge, and it has long been celebrated for its extreme beauty; while the *northern* entrance, down the avenue of trees in St Giles's, is almost equally so, and bears more resemblance to the Boulevards of Paris and some other foreign cities than to anything to which we are accustomed in England. The *southern* entrance also, over Folly Bridge, passing Christ Church College and the Town-hall, was far superior to the present disagreeable western approach.

These four ways meet in one centre (which the omnibus will probably pass) called Carfax, supposed to be a corruption of *Quatre-faces*, or *Quatre-voies*.

During the few moments which he has at his disposal, on the road to Christ Church—for there is little worth observation as he passes along—the visitor may well turn his thoughts to the early history of this great University.

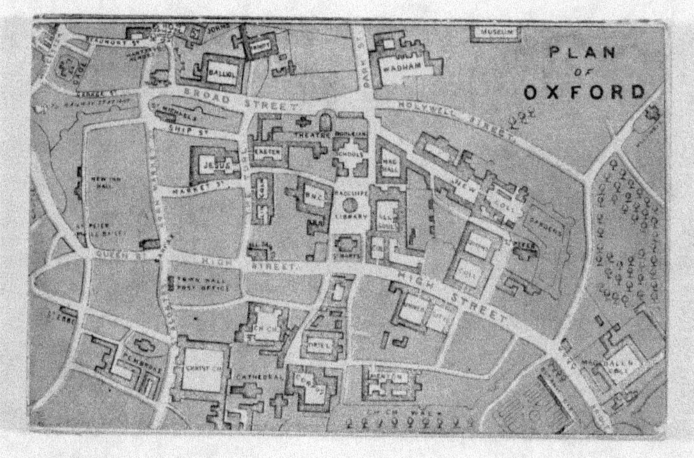

Howard Williams, 1875

Howard Williams (1854-1933) was born in Greenwich, son of a tobacco merchant. In 1875, with his two brothers and two friends, he set out by boat from Oxford to London (where Howard lived). His diary of their adventures (reminiscent of Jerome's *Three Men in a Boat*) was published in 1982 as *The Diary of a Rowing Tour from Oxford to London via Warwick, Gloucester, Hereford and Bristol.*

Saturday, July 31st

My brothers and I got up at six, and Fred came in soon after, and we all had breakfast together: we fetched a cab, and packed George and the luggage in it, started him off, and we three walked down to Paddington station. The station was crowded with people going off on excursions, this being the Saturday before Bank Holiday… We took a ticket for the boat, which cost 37/6d., and our own tickets, bought some papers, got a carriage to ourselves, started at 8.10, and had a very pleasant journey down Oxford. We saw the effects of the late floods, the county being covered sometimes for miles, and the tops of the hay-cocks in some places appearing above the water. We reached Oxford at 11.30, and found the station in a great state of confusion, crowded with country people evidently going off for their holidays. We waited about in the station for quite half an hour, our trucks being shunted about from one place to another. Eventually we saw them taken off into a siding, so leaving Fred in charge of the luggage, George, Tom and got hold of two porters, lifted the boat off the trucks, and carried it on our shoulders some little distance along the to line to where the railway over the River Cherwell; we then went down a little narrow path the embankment and launched it. Fred soon appeared with the luggage, and another porter with the sculls, cushions etc., and they were all placed in the boat. Fred and George then went into the town with one of the cans to get something to eat and drink, and also to obtain the Canal Pass, without which craft are not allowed to pass through the locks. George got this at the office, for which he had to pay 20/-, and Fred struck a bargain at a cook shop for some hot meat, which having wrapped up in a nice piece of paper he brought to us; he also bought some new loaves and some milk. In the meantime, Tom and I had not been idle, we had got the boat through a lock into the Oxford Canal along which lay our route; had put everything in order, and had got out the cheese preparatory to the arrival of the bread. On the arrival of George and Fred we partook of frugal but hearty repast.

The locks on this canal are all closed on Sunday, there being no traffic allowed on that day, and the lock keeper was just going home after fastening the gates, but we stopped him and he waited until we had passed through. We started on our journey at 1.30, there was a stiff breeze blowing, but it was a lovely afternoon with a bright warm sun.

Jerome K. Jerome, 1889

Jerome K. Jerome (1859–1927) was a writer best known of course for *Three Men in a Boat* (1889), a light-hearted travelogue about a return boat voyage from Kingston upon Thames to Oxford.

We spent two very pleasant days at Oxford. There are plenty of dogs in the town of Oxford. Montmorency had eleven fights on the first day, and fourteen on the second, and evidently thought he had got to heaven.

Among folk too constitutionally weak, or too constitutionally lazy, whichever it may be, to relish up-stream work, it is a common practice to get a boat at Oxford, and row down. For the energetic, however, the up-stream journey is certainly to be preferred. It does not seem good to be always going with the current. There is more satisfaction in squaring one's back, and fighting against it, and winning one's way forward in spite of it—at least, so I feel, when Harris and George are sculling and I am steering.

To those who do contemplate making Oxford their starting-place, I would say, take your own boat—unless, of course, you can take someone else's without any possible danger of being found out. The boats that, as a rule, are let for hire on the Thames above Marlow, are very good boats. They are fairly water-tight; and so long as they are handled with care, they rarely come to pieces, or sink. There are places in them to sit down on, and they are complete with all the necessary arrangements—or nearly all—to enable you to row them and steer them.

Reuben Gold Thwaites, 1891

Reuben Gold Thwaites (1853-1913) was an American historian and librarian whose parents came from Yorkshire. He made various canoe trips in the US, and in 1891 took the trip recalled in his 1892 book *Our Cycling Tour in England: from Canterbury to Dartmoor Forest, and back by way of Bath, Oxford and the Thames Valley.*

Saturday 2nd July

Our first view of Oxford, from the height at Cumnor, was just as the sun was sinking over the edge of the hills bordering the upper reaches of the Thames, which here describes an inverted V, the apex just beyond the sturdy Hill of Wytham to our north. Below us lay dark meadows, heavily clumped with trees, and over to the right the spires and towers of the ancient university town rising above a mass of greenery. To either side, tumbled hills were edging the fertile plain. At first deep and height were alike veiled in bluish mist, until a momentary rent in the angry storm-clouds now gathering in the west let forth imprisoned gleams of light which brought out each landscape line with sharp distinctness. Then the black mass, rebounding, effectually closed in upon this lurid splendor. As we mounted for our final coast, hill-tops and plain were covered with the pall of night.

Joseph Wells, 1898

Joseph Wells (1855–1929) was an author and Oxford academic (he was Vice-Chancellor from 1923–26). In this brief selection from his 1898 book *Oxford and its Colleges*, he reflects on a time of change.

Our own day has seen a complete change in Oxford. The new examination statute, which came in with the century, has stimulated industry and systematized work (the latter perhaps too much). The Oxford movement has revived the religious life of Oxford; the wave of democratic feeling has extended the sympathies of the University, and has, through two Commissions, carried out changes in the statutes, which often have paid little respect to the wishes of founders. Clerical restrictions have been almost entirely abolished, the marriage of fellows has been permitted, new subjects of study have been introduced and endowed, religious tests have been removed, even women have been admitted to the teaching (though not as yet to the degrees) of Oxford. It is fitting that so many and such rapid changes should be reflected in the new Oxford which our own generation has created; the University, and almost every College, has added largely to its buildings. Though there have been some cruel acts of vandalism, yet more often the additions are really gains to the beauty of Oxford. So we may hope that in spite of all changes, the best of the spirit of Oxford has been maintained, and that her sons, while reaching forward to the changes of the future, may yet prove not unworthy heirs of the treasures of the past.

Julia Clark Hallam, 1900

Julia Clark Hallam (1860–1927) was an American author and campaigner for votes for women; she was from Iowa. Her book *The Story of a European Tour* was published in 1900.

We had only planned one more stop in England before going to the "great city" — London. This stop was to be at the historic town of Oxford, whose world-wide reputation as a college center always attracts the American tourist. Besides the college, or rather the group of twenty colleges, which has made this English town so famous, it was the scene of the great religious conflict of the sixteenth century, which resulted in the burning at the stake of Bishops Latimer, Ridley and Cranmer. We were shown through St Mary's church, where these noted men were tried and condemned to death. It is here, also, that the unfortunate Amy Robsart, whose story has been made familiar to American readers through Scott's "Kenilworth," is said to be buried. These historical matters were faithfully expounded to us by a chubby little woman who was cleaning the church when we went in. In return for her information she gratefully pocketed the sixpence which was offered her.

Later we repaired to that street where the iron cross sunk into the pavement marks the identical spot where the bishops suffered martyrdom, while in a finely located position a short distance from the cross stands the beautiful monument which has been ‘erected to their memory. The monument is a tall, tower-like structure, upon the top of which, looking in three different directions, stand the figures of the three bishops. The name of each is inscribed below his form in letters so large that all who wish to read them may do so. The citizens of Oxford all seem familiar with the history connected with these memorials, and take great pride in pointing them out to the visitors.

To return to the college — one little incident in connection with our search for it will illustrate some of the difficulties of travelers, and at the same time illustrate the exceeding slowness with which some minds adjust themselves to an unfamiliar form of expression. We were exploring the town on foot, and at the same time making our way in what we supposed to be the direction of the college. We were in fact directly opposite one of the college buildings. So unlike a college did this building appear that we were constrained to ask a shopkeeper standing in front of his store if he would direct us to “Christ’s College.” He looked at us in blank amazement, shook his head and said there was no such building in town. We looked at each other and debated as to what was the matter with our question, for we knew we must be very near the building we were seeking. Finally it occurred to us that it was sometimes called “Christ’s Church College,” and we repeated our former question, putting in the word “church.” The face of the shopkeeper brightened up at once, and he pointed across the way to an expanse of dingy, discolored wall, which reminded me more of soldiers’ barracks than of college buildings. An old man was at the door who, for a compensation, would be glad to show us through all of the buildings and describe them to us. We accepted his services, and the next two hours were spent in wandering through the historic halls, chapels and galleries of old Oxford.

The different colleges are strung along together, the walls of one joining closely to the walls of that next to it. Each college is built around a beautifully kept quadrangle. We never could have understood just what the arrangement was if we had only obtained a view from the ground. But we climbed to the top of the "Camera," which is the reading room of the famous "Bodlian Library," where we obtained a beautiful and comprehensive view of all of the buildings, as well as of the rest of the city. I suppose that there exists nowhere upon this round earth literary relics and treasures of more intrinsic value than those which repose under the strictest watch and guard within the walls of the Bodlian Library. So precious are many of the things which are kept in the "Camera" that notices are kept posted about the building imposing the strictest fine and penalty upon any one who shall bring either fire or light into it. And this, too, although the building is composed entirely of stone and iron. One has to be exceedingly learned to appreciate the things which are found at Oxford. I felt that I knew very little, and wished that I could sit down and study about some of the things, but it is quite unnecesssary to say that I did not do this, for it was time to go to London.

Herbert Evans, 1905

Herbert Arthur Evans (1846–1923) was an English author and Shakespeare scholar who wrote two books in the popular Highways and Byways series of topographical guides for travellers, including *Highways and Byways in Oxford and the Cotswolds*, 1905.

… you take your seat in the express at Paddington, and have hardly scanned your newspaper through, when you are gliding past reservoirs and gas works into Oxford station. If the stranger is resolute enough to close his eyes at Kennington Island and refuse to open them till his cab deposits him at his hotel, he will be the happier man. Then let him ascend the roof of the Radcliffe, or, better still, walk to the top of Shotover, before he attempts to explore the city in detail.

But there are other distant views of Oxford besides that from Shotover. I have seen them all, and the best to my mind is the one (to be strictly accurate there is more than one, each with its special charm) from Stow Wood on the way to Beckley. If the day is a stormy one, and you are lucky enough to seize the moment when, from a rent in the black clouds which fill the valley and shroud the distant landscape, the sun breaks forth and lights up the towers and spires into bold relief, you will have seen a picture which you will never forget. From Stow Wood and Shotover your survey is from the north-east and west, but the famous view from the south must not be neglected, either from the meadow ground above the Hinkseys, or from the Abingdon Road, as you ascend to Boar's Hill; here, however, the suburbs assert their unblushing presence, and the foreground is more commonplace, but at my rate you see Oxford as it is from end to end, a city rising from the midst of a valley just at the point where the hills on either side, east and west, approach each other most nearly. It thus forms the gate through which all must pass who intend to accompany me into the land we are to explore in the present volume…

[Rowing on the rivers.]

… Cross the river in a punt and stroll down the towing-path, and you will have a good view of the practising eights and fours, as well as of sundry smaller craft. This will give you a good idea of Oxford "form" in its various stages of efficiency, but if you want to see it at its best, you must wait for the bumping races in February and May. The towing-path is then a less desirable point of observation, for it is crowded by an excited multitude, tearing along to keep pace with the competing boats, and cheering their crews not merely vocally, but by all such sounds of harmony as may be produced by rattles of large size, megaphones, and even pistol shots ; while if a bump be imminent, the air is rent by shouts that may be heard half a mile away; "Now you're gaining!" "Now put it on!" "Now you've got them! " "Well rowed, stroke!" "Keep it up, bow!" and so on. But I must not assume that the reader is initiated into the mysteries of Oxford boating, and he may very naturally wonder what a bump may be. I hasten therefore to explain that the river is not wide enough for more than two boats to start abreast, and that arrangements have to be made for at least a score. Each College has its own boat, and in the "Torpids" some colleges have two. Under these circumstances the problem is solved as follows: the several boats are posted in a long line at equal distances apart, the tail boat being close to Iffley Lock.

On the first day of the races, which last a week, the order of precedence is that of the final order resulting from the races of the previous year. At a given signal the boats start simultaneously, and it is the object of each to foul with its bows the stern of the one immediately ahead of it. This manoeuvre is the bump, and the next day the bumping boat takes precedence of the bumped. The February races are those of the junior crews or "Torpids"; the May races those of the senior crews or "Eights." The Eights are recruited from the Torpids, and the University Eight from the College Eights.

The May races are the great Oxford carnival: mothers, sisters, cousins, aunts come flocking in their hundreds; picnics, promenades, teas, dinners are the order of the day; even dances — long supposed the peculiar privilege of Commemoration week — have been heard of, and both entertainers and entertained may boast with Lord Foppington that life is an eternal round O of delights. But Eights' week or not Eights' week, summer term is the time for "the Joys of Oxford Living," the time for Panama hats and loose attire, the time for lounging in punts, or flirting in "Canaders." It may be that presently when we turn out of Mesopotamia into the Parks and saunter along the willowed margin of the "Cher," we may chance to spy Youth on the prow, and Pleasure at the helm gliding softly up towards distant Islip, babbling "of many things," but not unmindful of luncheon and of a descent upon the ripening meadow hay of some long suffering Marston farmer.

C.G. Harper, 1905

Charles George Harper (1863–1943) was an author and illustrator who wrote and illustrated around 170 travel books. This brief selection is from *The Oxford, Gloucester and Milford Haven Road*, 1905.

Although the chief coach inn of Oxford, the 'Angel' in High Street, has vanished, there still remains a very striking group of old coaching hostelries in Cornmarket Street…

The Cornmarket Inns are sadly dwindling. On one side is 'The Clarendon' (formerly 'Star') still unchanged from the day when the old 'Blenheim' coach drew up before its long stuccoed front. On the other, 'The Roebuck,' shouldered by 'The Golden Cross' — narrow entry, cobble stone yard, high gables, Jacobean windows of the belvedere or perpendicular oriel. Every line and curve of these old buildings and outhouses is a seventeenth-century lyric. It does the connoisseur of the roads good to see 'The Golden Cross' a going concern. To observe the joints, hanging up where joints have been hanged for four hundred years, and to see the long row of bells waggling and hear them jangling in the service of guests. There goes John, the Boots, busy in his department, down the yard, successor to a long line of such useful functionaries — I think he must be John the Thirtieth, or some such respectable number; and out of a window leans a saucy handmaiden, observing the arrival of a guest, just as the equally saucy Joans and Kates did when gay Cavaliers thronged the yard in those days when Oxford was held for the King.

Hippolyte Taine, 1871

Hippolyte Taine (1828–93) was a French historian and literary critic. He visited England on various occasions and lectured in Oxford in 1871. This note is from a letter to his wife, published in the 1908 translation *The Life and Letters of H. Taine*.

6 June. I have been working for two hours in the Bodleian Library, and at intervals strolling through the buildings and the quadrangles. They are building and planting here, as well as preserving the old. Keble College, for instance; and the University Museum, an enormous new building, Gothic, in staring brick, with pointed roof and ugly little cupolas like extinguishers, the roof, tiled blue and red alternately, giving a most unsatisfactory effect. Mr. Ruskin, who is a professor here, directed the construction of this museum; his books are better than his buildings. But the new park, with its vistas of green distance, its little hills lost in blue haze, will be quite charming in another hundred years. Nothing is more admirable than the way in which the future is here provided for.

C. Lewis Hind, 1908

C. Lewis Hind (1862–1927) was a journalist and art historian, whose *The Diary of a Looker-on* (1908) records an outsider's view of Oxford.

An unseen clock chimed the quarter before six. I was early for the service in Magdalen College Chapel, so I wandered through the quadrangles, loitered in the dim cloisters, and invited the salient impressions of that day in Oxford to visualise themselves…

Here, in this place of repose, and memories of Wolsey, Addison, and Gibbon, dominated by the Founders' Tower, where the Latin hymn is sung on May morning, the new and the old buildings united by the darkness, I was again conscious of the insistent impression that the stranger feels as he roams Oxford: the young life moving blithely against the grey and often peeling walls — ancestral buildings fostering infinite generations of children. You cannot escape the undergraduate. You do not wish to escape him. He is the butterfly of a day against an immemorial background. He is ubiquitous, ever busy, ever lively. He dresses carelessly and roughly as for a country walk, all but his waistcoat, which is always almost outrageous. Yet there must be a dandy set. Else how explain the vivid scarlet socks and the rainbow dressing-gowns in shop windows. The solemn night-gloom of Magdalen cloisters shrouded all colour, but life persisted. Beyond the arches, now here, now there, figures flitted, their gowns blown out by the wind, their feet skirting the lawns (those wonderful Oxford lawns); above them the old trees, and everywhere the spirit of the place brooding in the secrecy of the night. To the last frontier of Empire, Alma Mater breathes her benedictions upon her sons, remaining as much a part of them as their childhood.

And here am I, a stranger, trying to give an impression of Oxford in a page. Why, one college would overflow the space; one Hall of portraits; one wing of the Bodleian; one room of the University Galleries; one night at the Union; one dinner in the Hall; when the Eight, a little late, bounce in so vivid with vitality that they startle you like the shower of rockets at the end of Henley Week; one sight of a piece of venerable and lovely tapestry ('It was given to the College by Henry VIII,' remarked my informant casually); one grave Professor with a European reputation as a philosopher, seated at the High Table of his Hall at eight in the morning solemnly checking the butter, milk, and bread bills of his undergraduates…

It was a wrench to return to High Street, and to jump upon a tramcar, but the full moon hung over Magdalen Tower. Those voices still sounded in my ears as the train rushed towards London. I could not easily shake off the memory of Oxford… when I picked my way through the bustling streets of London, Great Tom was pealing the curfew, and the College gates were swinging into their locks.

Arthur Mee, 1942

Arthur Mee (1875–1943) was a prolific journalist and editor, author or editor of vast numbers of magazines and books, most notably *The Children's Encyclopedia* and the *King's England* series. The *Oxfordshire* volume of the latter was published in 1942, based on fieldwork before the Second World War, and the text below comes from the introduction.

Oxford has been treated in this book as a University city and little or no attention has been paid to the fact that it has unhappily allowed itself to be robbed of much of its beauty in recent years. In that it has suffered with all England, though in such a city the loss is grievous beyond words. Yet it is not entirely irreparable, and the Oxford Preservation Trust deserves the gratitude of the whole kingdom for its energetic efforts to reconstruct the city in keeping with its unique possessions and traditions. Oxford has allowed itself to be besmirched by industry and indifference, but the Trust has worked out plans which aim at transforming the city by keeping away the heavy industries, the control of lighter industries, the cleaning-up of the railway station area, the removal of the civic area from the crowded Carfax, the demolition of the prison, the lay-out of the Castle Mound as a garden, and so on. It is a plan full of promise, and as it commands the approval of all people of goodwill it is to be hoped that financial security will be forthcoming to save this famous city from the dead hand of its destroying generation.

The architectural student will find in Oxford all he wants, and he will probably begin with the famous Tower of the Five Orders from which a feeble king looks down on the intellectual world of the Bodleian. He will seek out the graceful arcades at St John's, and the masterpieces of Christopher Wren in the Sheldonian Theatre, and the Tom Tower at Christ Church. The gateway of Queen's is one of the best works of Wren's pupil Nicholas Hawksmoor… [also] successful was James Gibbs with his monumental Radcliffe Camera. Delightful, too, are some of Oxford's modern buildings: Rhodes House by Sir Herbert Baker, and the new buildings of the Bodleian and Lady Margaret Hall by Sir Giles Scott.

Index of Main Places

www.ingramcontent.com/pod-product-compliance
Lightning Source LLC
La Vergne TN
LVHW020045110826
845155LV00029B/638

* 9 7 8 1 9 0 5 3 1 5 3 7 6 *